Books by Michael Rosen

CENTRALLY HEATED KNICKERS

MICHAEL ROSEN'S A to Z: THE BEST CHILDREN'S
POETRY FROM AGARD TO ZEPHANIAH (Ed.)

MICHAEL ROSEN'S BIG BOOK OF BAD THINGS

MICHAEL ROSEN'S BOOK OF VERY
SILLY POEMS (Ed.)

NO BREATHING IN CLASS

QUICK, LET'S GET OUT OF HERE

YOU WAIT TILL I'M OLDER THAN YOU

MICHAEL ROSEN'S

A to Z

The BEST Children's Poetry from Agard to Zephaniah

Illustrated by Joe Berger

PUFFIN

For Emma, Elsie and Emile

PUFFIN BOOKS

Published by the Penguin Group
Penguin Books Ltd, 80 Strand, London WC2R ORL, England
Penguin Group (USA) Inc., 375 Hudson Street, New York, New York 10014, USA
Penguin Group (Canada), 90 Eglinton Avenue East, Suite 700, Toronto, Ontario, Canada M4P 2Y3
(a division of Pearson Penguin Canada Inc.)
Penguin Ireland, 25 St Stephen's Green, Dublin 2, Ireland (a division of Penguin Books Ltd)
Penguin Group (Australia), 250 Camberwell Road, Camberwell, Victoria 3124, Australia
(a division of Pearson Australia Group Pty Ltd)
Penguin Books India Pvt Ltd, 11 Community Centre, Panchsheel Park, New Delhi – 110 017, India
Penguin Group (NZ), 67 Apollo Drive, Rosedale, North Shore 0632, New Zealand
(a division of Pearson New Zealand Ltd)
Penguin Books (South Africa) (Pty) Ltd, 24 Sturdee Avenue, Rosebank, Johannesburg 2196, South Africa

Penguin Books Ltd, Registered Offices: 80 Strand, London WC2R ORL, England

puffinbooks.com

First published 2009
This edition published 2010
1

The acknowledgements on pages 275–285 constitute an extension of this copyright page.

Typeset in 13/16 pt Bembo MT Pro by Palimpsest Book Production Limited, Grangemouth, Stirlingshire
Made and printed in England by Clays Ltd, St Ives plc

British Library Cataloguing in Publication Data
A CIP catalogue record for this book is available from the British Library

ISBN: 978-0-141-33477-6

www.greenpenguin.co.uk

Contents

Foreword

A gang of poets has landed in your hand. We're talking, chanting, singing, dancing, shouting and whispering. Open any page and there we are. We're tall, we're short, we're loud, we're quiet. We're women, we're men. We're old, we're young. Some of us were born near you. Some of us were born far away. We all do one thing that is the same: we write and perform poems. But our poems are different. Our poems talk about a huge variety of things and we do it in many, many different ways.

One thing you can do with this book, is look at all the different things we write about, and all the different ways we write.

Another thing you can do with this book is take a poem and see what it sounds like when you say it. Or you could ask someone else to say it. Then you could have a go at doing it together. To do a poem together, you don't all have to say all the words. While one person is reading the poem, you could just sway to and fro to the rhythm of it. That's because poems don't just live in our brains. They live in our bodies. We can move our arms, our legs and our eyes when a poem is happening. We can shut our eyes and imagine the scenes and pictures that the poet is talking about. We can let ourselves wonder why one picture is next to another picture. So many pictures!

As you can see, this is an A to Z. And the great thing about an A to Z is that you don't have to start at the beginning and work through to the end if you don't want to. You can start where you want to, go backwards and forwards, round and round, looking for poems you like. And you'll always know where you are!

One problem: poets can be awkward people. For some letters we couldn't find a poet and none of the poets would change their names to fit one of the missing letters! So I've played about on those pages. Maybe you know someone who could be a poet for one of those pages. No – better still – why don't you make your own A to Z poetry book in your class, or in your school, or online with your friends?

One sad bit: my idea for this book came from shows I was doing with many of these poets. This book, I thought, would be for poets who are alive, now, living in Britain, who go out and perform their poems for people like you. You could get to see any of us sometime in your school or local library or in a theatre near you. And that is what you've got here. But then one of the poets died. That's Adrian Mitchell. He was someone we admired, loved and was a great friend and teacher to us. As you can imagine, I couldn't bear to take Adrian out of the book. I want him to be as alive as he can be, among the rest of us, remembered by his poems.

And in a way, that's what poems are: little parcels of memory, little packages of what a poet has thought or wondered about or seen and heard. And then by putting them on a page in a book, the poems can sit there for years and years and years, ready for people like you to unpack, take out and enjoy. Yes – enjoy!

Michael Rosen

Spellbound

Ride with me
On this lyrical roller coaster
My syllable slices
Will feed your hunger
As they pop up and down
Like a Jamaican toaster

Chilling in my simile cocoon
Just biding my time
The moment is perfect
Let's get ready to rhyme

Watch your step
As my Webb is spun
Drop your baggage at check in
The lighter you travel
The more fun

Submerge yourself, in this
Lip-hop metaphor
Resistance is futile,
As I hold the key to the door

I leave you tongue-tied like Houdini
You'll never escape my barrel of words

Your belly expands with laughter
As you guzzle on my contagious verbs

My acid adjectives
Hack deep into your heart
Reprogramming your software
Be afraid!
Be very afraid
For this is just the start

You'll be my reluctant patient
And I'll play the over enthusiastic nurse
Drip feeding rhythm and rhyme
Through my life saving verse

Bringing forth gifts of expression
With the knowledge of 3 wise men
Verbalizm is the one Like Nio
Now five plus four equals ten

Verbalizm is the ultimate fighter
A lion that can't be tamed
A fusion of text and colour
This canvas is too big to be framed

There'll be no light limericks
This operation is far too serious for that
Lights, camera, action!

Cut! . . .
Now that's what I call a Rap!

Ad–libbing like a master chef
Preparing food, to serenade the nose
One whiff of this concoction
Leaves you spellbound, by my Moorish prose

ADISA

Chick Pea Pie

In the food bacchanal
Food just a jam; to the steel pan
No humans in sight
Strictly vegetables deh pon the street
Tonight

I see rice a jump high
Somersaulting in the wind
Kidney peas too fat to jump
Her belly just a drag pon the floor

Chick peas swimming in an ocean of curry
Plantain a sunbathe skin turn black in the sun
Green banana, making eyes at cho cho
Him say, "Tonight I must get that one"

Aubergine a whine she waist
Putting a smile on
Dashin and yam face
Two bad bwoys
Who never skin teeth
When them see aubergine
Them ball "what a girl look sweet"

Spinach and cousin callaloo
A try fe tease black eye peas

Spinach flutter her eyelashes
Black eye peas body start to swell
Callaloo blow peas a kiss
I think I am in Love
Peas start fe YELL

Okra a chat to
Big belly breadfruit
About the good old years
That passed them by

Breadfruit rub him charcoal belly
And lift him head to the sky
Okra skin is no longer furry
Her insides are scaly and dry

What has become of our youth?
How fast life has passed us by
Observing the others next to them
Aubergine plantain and yam
Tears swelled up in their eyes
For tonight after the carnival
They would all surely die
For tomorrow Mama will cook them
In her famous
Chick Pea Pie.

ADISA

The Soldiers Came

The soldiers came
and dropped their bombs.
The soldiers didn't take long
to bring the forest down.

With the forest gone
the birds are gone.
With the birds gone
who will sing their song?

But the soldiers forgot
to take the forest
out of the people's hearts.
The soldiers forgot
to take the birds
out of the people's dreams.
And in the people's dreams
the birds still sing their song.

Now the children
are planting seedlings
to help the forest grow again.
They eat a simple meal of soft rice
wrapped in banana leaf.

And the land welcomes their smiling
like a shower of rain.

JOHN AGARD

Laughter Rap in Plastic Town

One day as I was passing through plastic town
I happened to pass a school playground
yet I couldn't hear one laughing sound.

Can you imagine a school playground
and not a single laughing sound?
But that's how it was in plastic town.

For though they were playing as children play,
plastic children do so in a most unusual way.
Not one was laughing, not one I say.

Every move they made was made of plastic
it was sad to see children so robotic.
They could do with a touch of my laughing magic.

So I reached for my hip-hop cap
got into my egg-leg tap
broke into my laughing rap.

Children, children of plastic town
it makes me sad to see you frown.
Cracking up with laughter is the thing to do,

cracking up with laughter makes you feel brand-new.
So give me a crick, give me a crack,
just throw yourself into the laughing act.

I promise my magic will bring you right back.

JOHN AGARD

The Mighty Slide

The snow has fallen in the night.
The temperature's exactly right.
The playground's ready, white and wide;
Just waiting for the mighty slide.

The first to arrive is Denis Dunne.
He takes a little stuttering run.
Sideways he slides across the snow;
He moves about a yard or so,
With knees just bent and arms out wide;
And marks the beginning of the slide.

Then Martin Bannister appears,
His collar up around his ears,
His zipper zipped, his laces tied,
And follows Denis down the slide.
The snow foams up around their feet,
And melts, too, in the friction's heat.
It changes once, it changes twice:
Snow to water; water to ice.

Now others arrive: the Fisher twins
And Alice Price. A queue begins.
The slide grows longer, front and back,
Like a giant high-speed snail's track.

And flatter and greyer and glassier, too;
And as it grows, so does the queue.
Each waits in line and slides and then
Runs round and waits and slides again.

And little is said and nothing is planned,
As more and more children take a hand
(Or a foot, if you like) in the slide's construction.
They work without wages and minus instruction.
Like a team of cleaners to and fro
With clever feet they polish the snow.
Like a temporary tribe in wintry weather,
They blow on their gloves and pull together.

A dozen children, maybe more,
All skidding on the frozen floor.
The brave, like bulls, just charge the ice,
And one of these is Alice Price;
Her red scarf flying in the breeze,
You'd think she had a pair of skis.
Others approach more cautiously;
Denis for one (though he wouldn't agree).
His wobbly style is unmistakable:
The sign of a boy who knows he's breakable.

And now the slide is really growing,
And the rhythm of the queue is flowing.
Some keep a place or wait for a friend,
Some dive in the snow when they reach the end,

Some slide and pretend to be terrified,
Some stand in the queue and *never* slide.

There are children with bags and children without,
As they roll the silver carpet out;
And some in pairs and some in a bunch,
And one or two *eating*: an early lunch.
There's flying hair and frozen feet,
And big and little, and scruffy and neat.
There's shouting and shoving: 'Watch this!' 'Watch me!'
'I'm floating!' 'I'm falling!' 'Oh, Mother!' 'Wheee!'
And all the while from the frosty ground
That indescribable *sliding* sound.
Yes, snow's a pleasure and no mistake,
But the slide is the icing on the cake.

'If we knocked that wall down, moved that shed,
We could slide for miles!' the children said.
'If we knocked it *all* down – wallop – bop –
We could slide for ever and never stop!'
An icy ribbon tidily curled
In a giant circle round the world.

The slide by now is forty feet long,
And a number of things have begun to go wrong.
The queue stretches back to the playground gate;
Certain boys find it hard to wait.

While tough boys like Hoskins or Kenny Burns
Are simply not *used* to taking turns.
Like pockets of chaos or bits of sin,
They break up the queue and muscle in.

And all the time the slide gets slicker,
And the sliders slide along it quicker.
The quickest by far is Frankie Slater:
'When I grow up I'll be a skater!'
The craziest? Well, Colin Whittle;
He thinks the boy in front is a skittle.
There are bumps and bruises, bets and dares,
Cries, collisions, pile-ups, *prayers*!

But even worse than damaged kids,
The slide itself is on the skids.
The feet that brought it to perfection
Are pushing it now in a different direction.
For everything changes, that much is true;
And a part of the playground is poking through.

'It's wearing away!' 'It's wearing out!'
'We need more snow!' the children shout.
At which point Hoskins quietly swears,
And – minus the coat he never wears –
Raises his hand like a traffic cop
And calls on his fellow sliders to stop.

Then straight away from the ranks of the queue
Step Denis and Martin and Alice, too.
With no one to tell them and no one to ask,
They tackle the urgent chilly task.
They scoop the snow from either side
And bandage up the poorly slide.
Tread on it, trample it, smooth it, thump it.
'If that don't work, we'll have to jump it!'
'Jump what?' says Denis, looking queasy.
'The gap!' says Alice. 'Easy-peasy!'

Elsewhere in the playground, the usual scene:
A teacher on duty, it's Mrs Green.
A huddle of (mostly) shivering mums;
Some wondering babies, sucking thumbs
(Watching the world from way behind
As they wait in a queue of a different kind).
A gang of girls, they're shivering, too,
Discussing who'll be friends with who.
A little infant darting about,
Giving his birthday invites out.
While scattered here and there besides,
Half a dozen smaller slides.
Snowball battles, snowball chases,
Swimming kit and violin cases:
A student with a tiger skin,
And *fourteen* children to carry it in.

The slide, meanwhile, with its cold compress,
Restored to health, well, more or less,
Remains by far the star attraction,
As Denis and Co. glide back into action.
With breath like smoke and cheeks like roses,
Pounding hearts and runny noses,
Eyes a-sparkle, nerves a-quiver,
Not a chance of a chill or a sign of a shiver
(It's a funny thought, that – it's nice – it's neat:
A thing made of ice and it generates heat),
They slide and queue and slide again;
There's six in a line – no, seven – no, ten!

A motley crew, a happy band,
Attending their own strip of land.
'Fifty foot long by two foot wide!'
'By half an inch thick!' – that's the mighty slide.
Cool and grey and, now, complete.
A work of art, all done by feet.

Then, suddenly, a whistle blows,
And all the human dynamos
(With outstretched arms and just-bent knees)
Skid to a halt, fall silent, freeze.
They stand in a trance, their hot breath steaming;
Rub their eyes as though they've been dreaming,
Or are caught in the bossy whistle's spell,
Or simply weary – it's hard to tell.

A few of them shiver, the air feels cool;
And the thought sinks in: it's time for school.

A little while later, observe the scene,
Transformed by a whistle and Mrs Green:
The empty playground, white and wide;
The scruffy snow, the silent slide.

Inside, with a maths card just begun
And his thoughts elsewhere, sits Denis Dunne.
His hands are chapped, his socks are wet,
But in his head he's sliding yet.
He sits near a window, he stares through the glass.
The teacher frowns from the front of the class.
Can this boy move! Can this boy skate!
'Come on, Denis – concentrate!'
Yes, nothing changes, that much is true,
And the chances of sliding in classrooms are few.
So Denis abandons his speculation,
And gets on with his education.

Some plough the land, some mow or mine it;
While others – if you let them – shine it.

ALLAN AHLBERG

I Speak the Language

I speak the language of Hello to English.
I speak the language of Bonjour to French.
I speak the language of Willow to Weeping.
I speak the language of Park to Bench.

I speak the language of Ni hao to Mandarin.
I speak the language of Hola to Spanish.
I speak the language of BingBam! to my Tambourine.
I speak the language of Munch to my Sandwich.

I speak the language of Jambo to Swahili.
I speak the language of Tasleemat to Urdu.
I speak the language of Splash! to Swimming.
I speak the language of Baby to Peek-a-boo!

I speak the language of Czesc to Polish.
I speak the language of Marhaba to Arabic.
I speak the language of Dreams to my Pillow.
I speak the language of Games to Olympic.

I speak the language of Rivers to Silver.
I speak the language of Sunshine to Gold.
I speak the language of Me to my Mirror.
I speak the language of Home to my World.

What languages do you speak?

FRANCESCA BEARD

GRRRR

If you smile then I will glare,
If you're sad then I don't care,
If you tell me I've been bad, I will say 'Oh
    good, I'm glad!'

I don't want to, I don't like you!
If you touch me, I will bite you!

If you try to calm me down, I will roll round
    on the ground.
If you try to make me stop, I will scream until
    I pop.
If you shh me, I will yell and yeLL and yELL
    and YELL and YELL!

I don't want to, I don't like you!
If you touch me, I will bite you!

If you try to make me eat, I'll spit my food out
    on the floor,
If you try to make me sleep, I'll bang my head
    against the door.
If you sing a lullaby, I'll join in the key of Y!

I don't want to, I don't like you!
If you touch me, I will bite you!

I'm the worst there's ever been, I'm the worst
    you've ever seen,
I'm a single-handed RIOT!!!!!!!!!!!!!!!!!!!!!!!!!!!!!!!
    !!!!!!!!!!!!!!!!!!!!!!!!!!!!!!!

(Now I'm ready to be quiet)

FRANCESCA BEARD

Jamaican Song

Little toad little toad mind yourself
mind yourself let me plant my corn
plant my corn to feed my horse
feed my horse to run my race –
the sea is full of more than I know
moon is bright like night time sun
night is dark like all eyes shut
     Mind – mind yu not harmed
     somody know bout yu
     somody know bout yu

Little toad little toad mind yourself
mind yourself let me build my house
build my house to be at home
be at home till I one day vanish –
the sea is full of more than I know
moon is bright like night time sun
night is dark like all eyes shut
     Mind – mind yu not harmed
     somody know bout yu
     somody know bout yu

JAMES BERRY

Okay, Brown Girl, Okay

For Josie, nine years old, who wrote to me saying, 'Boys called me names because of my colour. I felt very upset . . . my brother and sister are English. I wish I was, then I won't be picked on . . . How do you like being brown?'

Josie, Josie, I am okay
being brown. I remember,
every day dusk and dawn get born
from the loving of night and light
who work together, like married.
   And they would like to say to you:
   Be at school on and on, brown Josie
   like thousands and thousands and thousands
   of children, who are brown and white
   and black and pale-lemon colour.
   All the time, brown girl Josie is okay.

Josie, Josie, I am okay
being brown. I remember,
every minute sun in the sky
and ground of the earth work together
like married.
   And they would like to say to you:
   Ride on up a going escalator
   like thousands and thousands and thousands
   of people, who are brown and white

and black and pale-lemon colour.
All the time, brown girl Josie is okay.

Josie, Josie, I am okay
being brown. I remember,
all the time bright-sky and brown-earth
work together, like married
making forests and food and flowers and rain.
And they would like to say to you:
Grow and grow brightly, brown girl.
Write and read and play and work.
Ride bus or train or boat or aeroplane
like thousands and thousands and thousands
of children, who are brown and white
and black and pale-lemon colour.
All the time, brown girl Josie is okay.

JAMES BERRY

Air Raids 1942

And waking in the night I used to hear
The trains at King's Cross, shunting in the dark,
The clash and clank of buffers, clear as clear,
And, carried on the black night air, the rush of steam,
While everybody slept. No raid tonight.

And perhaps some boy in Hamburg woke as well,
And heard his father in a neighbouring room
Quietly talking on, or radio static.
In London I heard footsteps sometimes in the street.
Perhaps he heard some too. Or aeroplanes.

GERARD BENSON

Lost Gloves

They don't come out till the winter months
But stay in hiding. Then slowly one by one
They show themselves, dangling from railings,
Sitting on the tops of posts and pillar boxes,
Settling, fingers spread, on walls and fences;
Or simply lying on pavements or in parks.
   Gloves. Leather Gloves, woollen or cotton,
   Brown or black, blue, pink or holly-green,

Sometimes their fingers are inside-out
Or bent back. Sometimes they're crumpled,
Sometimes frozen into a pointing shape.
There's never more than one. Never a pair.
The lone gloves. The lost gloves. But look:
Here comes a kid, looking quite warm,
   And look at those gloves: one red mitten
   And one grey woollen, rather too large.

GERARD BENSON

In Daylight Strange

It was last Friday at ten to four I
Thought of the lion walking into the playground.
I was sitting, thinking, at our table when
The thought of the lion simply came,
And the sun was very hot, and the lion
Was in the yard (in daylight strange, because
Lions go out at night). He was
An enormous, sudden lion and he
Appeared just like that and was crossing very
Slowly the dusty playground, looking
To neither side, coming towards the door. He was
Coloured a yellow that was nearly grey, or a
Grey that was nearly yellow. He was so
Quiet that only I could hear the huge feet
Solidly pacing, and at the playground door he
Stopped, and looked powerfully in. There was
A forest following him, out in the street,
And noises of parakeets. When he stopped,
Looking like a picture of a lion in the frame
Of the open door, his eyes looked on at
Everything inside with a stern, curious look, he
Didn't seem completely to understand. So
He waited a second or two before
He roared. All the reeds on the river bank
Trembled, a thousand feet
Scattered among the trees, birds rose in clouds

But no one jumped in the classroom, no one screamed,
No one ran to ring the firebell, and
Miss Wolfenden went on writing on the board.
It was just exactly as if
They hadn't heard at all, as if nobody had heard.
And yet I had heard, certainly,
Yes. I had heard,
And I didn't jump.
And would you say you were surprised? Because
You ought not to be surprised.
Why should I be frightened when it was
Because *I* thought of the lion, that the lion was there?

ALAN BROWNJOHN

Elephant

It is quite unfair to be
obliged to be so large, so I suppose
you could call me discontented.

Think big, they said, when
I was a little elephant; they
wanted to get me used to it.

It was kind. But it doesn't help if,
inside, you are carefree in small ways,
fond of little amusements.

You are smaller than me, think
how conveniently near the flowers are,
how you can pat the cat by just

halfbending over. You can also
arrange teacups for dolls, play
marbles in the proper season.

I would give anything to be
able to do a tiny, airy, flitting
dance to show how very little a

thing happiness can be really.

ALAN BROWNJOHN

Tree

A tree
is not like you and
me – it waits around quite
patiently – catching kites and
dropping leaves – reaching out to touch
the breeze…A tree all day will stand and stare
clothed in summer, winter : bare – it has no shame
or modesty…Perhaps its generosity is the greatest in
the world – it gives a home to every bird, every squirrel,
feeds them too – to every dog it is a loo…And after dark
what does it do? Catch a falling star or two? Shimmy
in the old moonlight? Or maybe have a conker fight?
A tree can give an awful lot : the wood to make a
baby's cot – pencils, paper, tables, chairs – lolly
sticks as well as stairs …Without a tree we
could not live – a tree, it seems just
loves to give –
but us :
we
chop
we
take
we
burn
that's
what we
do in return

JAMES CARTER

35

What Can You Do With a Football?

Well . . .

You can
kick it you can catch
it you can bounce it – all
around. You can grab it you can
pat it **you can roll it** – on the ground.
You can throw it you can head it **you
can hit it** – with a bat. You can biff it
you can boot it you can spin it
you can shoot it you can drop it
you can stop it – **just
like that!**

JAMES CARTER

The Cancan

When I dance
my blood runs like a river can,
my feet fly like the birds can,
my heart beats like a drum can.
Because when I dance I can,
can do anything
when I dance.

Flying over rooftops
I see my town below me
where everybody knows me,
where all my problems throw me,
where heavy feet can slow me.
But nobody can, can stop me
when I dance.

My blood runs a race.
My feet fly in space.
My heart beats the pace.
Because when I dance I can,
can do anything
when I dance.

MANDY COE

Soft as the Blanket

If I touch a coin I can tell you
if it's heads or if it's tails.
I can taste a loaf of bread and swear
the baker wore blue shoes.
Say a daft thing
and make me grin,
I'm as soft as the blanket
you wrapped me in.

One silver raindrop on my tongue
and I feel the height of its fall.
If I brush a feather along my wrist
I know the miles it flew.
Say a daft thing
and make me grin,
I'm as soft as the blanket
you wrapped me in.

If I touch my lips to a stem of grass
I know what hour it was cut.
If I smell a yellow pencil
I'll tell you the last word it wrote.
Say a daft thing
and make me grin,
I'm as soft as the blanket
you wrapped me in.

I can taste in a grain of salt
the whale-songs of the sea.
If I touch your head I know
the colour of your dreams.
Say a daft thing
and make me grin,
I'm as soft as the blanket
you wrapped me in.

MANDY COE

39

Waht?

At frsit sghit tihs peom
May seem imosspbile to raed
Touhgh, as soon as you aemttpt to
You will esilay scceued.

And fnid you udnersatnd it
And aslo taht it ryhems.
Athluogh, it mghit mkae you dzizy
If you raed it sverael tmies.

PETER COLE

Brothers

Big
Strong
Billy
Matthews
Is
Very
Very
Tall,
Which
Makes
Him
Perfectly
Suited
For
Playing
Basketball.

Though his brother who is short
Is also good at sport.

PETER COLE

Let No one Steal Your Dreams

Let no one steal your dreams
Let no one tear apart
The burning of ambition
That fires the drive inside your heart

Let no one steal your dreams
Let no one tell you that you can't
Let no one hold you back
Let no one tell you that you won't

Set your sights and keep them fixed
Set your sights on high
Let no one steal your dreams
Your only limit is the sky

Let no one steal your dreams
Follow your heart
Follow your soul
For only when you follow them
Will you feel truly whole

Set your sights and keep them fixed
Set your sights on high
Let no one steal your dreams
Your only limit is the sky

PAUL COOKSON

Our Teacher is a Tongue Twister

Our teacher's strangest feature
Is his tongue that's strong and long
Like a big red carpet it unrolls
And what we like the most
Is when he's feeling gross
He sticks it out and shoves it up his nose

We can see it slide and squirm
Like a wibbly dribbly worm
Oozing slime and drooling where it goes
But his bestest ever trick
Is the one that makes us sick
When he sticks it out and shoves it up his nose

You can see around his lips
The sticky trail that drips
A pink and fatty slug that grows and grows
But if we're bored in class
He can always make us laugh
When he sticks it out and shoves it up his nose

Our long tongue twisting teacher's tongue
Is like an alien creature

A shell–less slimy snail that shows and glows
He just cannot resist it
The urge to turn and twist it
When he sticks it out and shoves it up his nose

And his nostrils open very wide . . .
And his tongue comes down the other side

PAUL COOKSON

Evening Shifts

As cloak-black clouds
of evening drift
across his torch-white eye,

the moon begins
his evening shift—
nightwatchman of the sky.

GRAHAM DENTON

'M'

My younger brother is learning his letters with
   my mum.
They're doing the 'M' sound.
Mum says, 'So,
how many words can you tell me
that begin with a "M"?'
And my younger brother says,
'M for . . . mountain.'
'Good,' says Mum.
'M for . . . monster.'
'That's right,' says Mum.
'M for . . . magic.'
'Well done!' says Mum. 'Any more?'
'*And* mummy begins with a M, too,'
my younger brother adds, proudly.
'Of course!' says Mum,
'But do you know what daddy begins with?'
   she asks.
'Yes,' my younger brother says,
'A cough and a splutter every morning.'

GRAHAM DENTON

First Gift

Don't expect a silver spoon from me.
I would give you this instead.

A coral spoon from Turkey, fished out
of the Marmara sea where mermaids
dined off dolphins' backs, flicking iridescent tails.

A well-used wooden spoon from Russia,
scarred by banging against a table, bean
and barley flying past the infant's crumpled face.

A spoon discovered in Iceland, carved
from horn and frozen in a spoke of frost, lost
when the Queen of the Mountain tried to feed the Beast.

A shell spoon from Macedonia, a dipper from Peru,
from Fiji a ladle made of the magic kava kava root
known to stir stories out of earth and air.

Each one fed another mouth
and had good daily use.

Of all the riches in the world
I would give you only this,
a simple way to know their lips,

to touch the hands
that handed on
the hand-me-down.

IMTIAZ DHARKER

The Day the Marks Made Sense

When my finger pushed at the marks
jumbled on a page and stumbled
on the world g i r l, when I found
that every scratch had its own sound
g
i
r
l
I said it in Scottish, 'girril'.

That was just the start. Words
made stories that flew out of books.
Buses had routes and I could
read them. Signs spoke to me
as if they had voices. I sent
messages, word came back.

Then the glass blue days began.
Bells found tongues and spoke.
as if they would never crack
or break. Now look, the marks made
birdflight. They are writing a song
out of the ground all the way across the sky.

IMTIAZ DHARKER

If You Were a Carrot

If you were a carrot
and I was a sprout
I'd boil along with you
I'd sit on your plate

If you were a tadpole
and I was a frog
I'd wait till your legs grew
I'd teach you to croak

If you were a conker
and I was a string
we'd win every battle
we'd beat everything

If you were a jotter
and I was a pen
I'd write you a message
again and again

If you were a farmer
I'd be in your herd
if you were a popsong
I'd sing every word

I wish I could tell you
that I like you a lot
but you're like a secret
and I'm like a knot.

BERLIE DOHERTY

Mushrooms

are bald.

They thrust their heads through soil
and commune
pale and quiet
in their own damp smell

Their stems pop when they're plucked
their skin peels away
their peat-cool flesh is soft

In hot-butter fry
they grow plump as the slugs
that slithered round their stems
they gleam with oozed sweat

And when they're bitten
they burst
spilling juices
that taste of grass
and dew trodden by horses
and foxy woodland
badgers at dusk
and the rich moist brown deep earth.

BERLIE DOHERTY

Rooty Tooty

Grandad used to be a pop star,
with a red–and–silver guitar.
He wore leather jackets and drainpipe jeans.
He drove around in limousines,
waving to screaming fans.
Fab! said Grandad. *Groovy!*
I really dig it, man!

Grandad used to have real hips,
he swivelled and did The Twist.
His record went to Number One.
Grandad went like this:
Rooty tooty, yeah yeah.
Rooty tooty, yeah yeah.
Rooty tooty, yeah yeah.
Then Grandad met Gran.

Gran was dancing under a glitterball.
Grandad was on bass.
He noticed how a thousand stars
sparkled and shone in her face.
And although Gran fancied the drummer,
Grandad persevered. He wrote Gran
a hundred love songs
down through their happy years.

Grandad used to be a pop star,
a rock'n'roll man –
Rooty tooty, yeah yeah yeah –
and Grandad loved groovy Gran.

CAROL ANN DUFFY

Your Dresses

I like your rain dress,
its strange, sad colour,
its small buttons like tears.

I like your fog dress,
how it swirls around you
when you dance on the lawn.

Your snow dress I like,
its million snowflakes
sewn together with a needle of ice.

But I love your thunderstorm dress,
its huge, dark petticoats,
its silver stitches flashing as you run away.

CAROL ANN DUFFY

Nathaniel

Nathaniel woke up yawning,
'I'm half asleep,' he said,
So his left half went down to breakfast
And his right half stayed in bed.

RICHARD EDWARDS

Finding Out About the Family

It was really rather scary
When my dear old Auntie Mary
Started going very hairy
When the moon was full and bright,
And went outside on the prowl
With a loud and eerie howl
Like a wild wolf on a hilltop
In the middle of the night.

It was really rather odd
When I found my Uncle Tod
Dangling from a wooden rod
Where a curtain usually hangs,
He was upside down, in black,
With his hair slicked thinly back,
And the firelight flickering fiercely
On the sharp tips of his fangs.

It was most bizarre of all
When my little brother Paul
Disappeared into the wall
In a puff of purple smoke,
Then my sister waved her wand,

And now I'm living in this pond
Eating flies and feeling slimy . . .
Ribbit ribbit, croak croak croak.

RICHARD EDWARDS

Dino's Café

In the café owned by Dino
Ye can hae a cappuccino,
For wee Dino's kettle's never aff the bile;
    And he'll serve ye mince and tatties,
    Macaroni and ciabatties,
    While he skites about his café wi a smile.

Dino dreams o hame in Naples
As he peels a pun o aipples
Wi his Scots-Italian flags up on the waw;
While he's weel-kent for his coffee,
His Tartan Pizza's rarely awfie,
And his Tutti Frutti Clooties ayewis braw.

In a brichtly-coloured peenie
Dino redds up a panini,
And he dichts doon aw the tables wi a cloot;
But when puir auld Auntie Betty
Got jurmummled in spaghetti,
Ten big fireman had tae come and cut her oot.

MATTHEW FITT

The Twins

Cammy Smith is ten year auld.
Wee Joe is his twin brither.
But naebody in Skooshy Kirk
Wid say they're like each ither.

When yin o them is stervin,
The ither's wame is steched.
When yin is fou o runnin,
The ither wan is peched.

Yin will burst oot greetin
If the ither tells a joke.
Yin will slerp and swallae
If the ither's gaun tae boak.

If Cammy fancies haggis,
The Joey jist wants neeps.
Yin's up watchin telly
While the ither brither sleeps.

On Monday, Cammy's clingin
While wee Joe's neat and trig.
Nixt day, Cammy's gleamin
But Joe's a clorty pig.

The boys are ayewis lauchin
But they never lauch thegither.
They're like that man and wifie
That tells the toun the weather.

MATTHEW FITT

Immigration Trap

Farida's mum is being sent home.
But Farida's allowed to stay.
Farida doesn't want her to go.
But Farida doesn't have a say.

Farida's lived here all her life.
She's British, like you and me.
But Farida's mum came here
As a stateless refugee.

And now the people who make the rules
Say Farida's mum must go
Back to the land she left
Twelve long years ago.

Back to a troubled land
Where people live in fear.
She has outstayed her welcome.
She is not wanted here.

But because Farida was born here,
Farida's allowed to stay.
She doesn't want her mum to go,
But she doesn't have a say.

JOHN FOSTER

Aunty Joan

When Aunty Joan became a phone,
She sat there not saying a thing.
The doctor said, shaking his head,
'You'll just have to give her a ring.'

We had a try, but got no reply.
The tone was always engaged.
'She's just being silly,' said Uncle Billy.
Slamming down the receiver enraged.

'Alas, I fear,' said the engineer,
Who was called in to inspect her,
'I've got no choice. She's lost her voice.
I shall have to disconnect her.'

The phone gave a ring. 'You'll do no such thing,'
Said Aunty's voice on the line.
'I like being a phone. Just leave me alone
Or else I'll dial nine, nine, nine!'

JOHN FOSTER

On Port Meadow

That horse looks bigger than a sofa
And its nose is damp as a dish-cloth.
One minute it was over there, nibbling grass,
And now it is here, nudging my shoulder.

The wind is blowing the kites away
And lacing the surface of the flooded field.
The seven horses who were minding their
   own business
Are now over here, looking for sugar-lumps.

It's no good laughing, and twisting away
Like Blind-Man's-Buff or a flamenco dancer:
The horses are all round us, snorting,
And one of them has bitten my Mum's bum.

JOHN FULLER

Insect Day

Miss told us we needn't go to school today
    Because it's Insect Day.
Miss told us we could stay at home and play
    Because it's Insect Day.
When she told us, we all shouted: "Hurray!"
And made a bee-line for the door. "Hurray! Hurray!"
    "It's Insect Day!"

But Miss said: "Sorry, it's not till Friday,
    So come back to your seats this instant
And clear up your things. I want the classroom tidy."
    She was smiling, but really quite insistent,
    Because of Insect Day.

"Don't think for a moment you're making a getaway.
    Friday is Insect Day
And although for you lot it may be a holiday,
    Your teachers have to stay.
So I don't want a mess. I'm not clearing it up, and hey!
That goes for you, too, buttercup. No way!"

I hope they enjoy their day of school
    On Insect Day.
I hope they listen and don't play the fool
    On Insect Day.
What, I wonder, will all the insects do?

Will they all turn up with their tiny school bags
	On Insect Day?
Will they put up their feelers to go to the loo?
And will Miss call them "little scallywags"
	On Insect Day?
Will they sit in our desks, with scabs on their six knees,
And buzz about in the playground during break
	On Insect Day?
Wasps and dragonflies, and ladybirds and bees?
Will the beetles find it hard to keep awake
	On Insect Day?

Think of roll-call:
David Aphid? Present!
Abdul Mosquito? Present!
Katy Katydid? Present!
Chuck Cicada? Present!
Anthea Ant? Present!
Eric Earwig? Present!
All present, all eager to learn!

But how can they learn anything in a single day?
Some of them barely live that long, and surely they
Don't *need* to read, or know how to model clay?
But I don't mind, if it means a holiday.

Miss told us we needn't go to school today
	Because it's Insect Day.

Miss told us we could stay at home and play
    Because it's Insect Day.

At least, that's what I heard her say.

JOHN FULLER

The Pool

We wade through corn like tigers on fire,
And run the obstacle course of barbed wire,
To follow the stream in a winding dream,
Until in a corner, scooped like ice cream,
Under the alders, a hidden pool,
I trail my fingers in the willowy cool.
The grass is bullied and nettles beaten,
Blankets laid for food to be eaten
We leap like salmon one, two, three,
Divebombers of this inland sea,
Hit the water, bodies froze,
Suddenly trout are tickling toes,
The oak is a mast in the ship of shade
Cows drift through the glassy glade
Heads bent like old men reading the news,
As beyond, the hills hold distant views
Under the beaming fat lady sun,
Witch of warmth, conjuring fun,
Until she grows tired and a little bit low,
And daylight packs up, ready to go!
Oh why can't summer last forever,
And why can't we take home this river?
In twilight we stumble through itchy corn,
Get caught on barbed wire with trousers torn,
Sleepily falling into cars
To carry us home under rippling stars.

ANDREW FUSEK PETERS

Attack of the Mutant Mangos: A Fruit Salad Ballad of Baddies

They are totally bananas
They hang out in a bunch
Don't trifle with these fruitcakes
Una-peeling, out to lunch
They'll orange a nasty accident
And prune you down to size
With hands around your neck-tarine
You'll end up in their pies.
They're evil, they're extrawberry
And rotten to the core,
No more pudding up with them
This is no food fight, it's a war!

ANDREW FUSEK PETERS

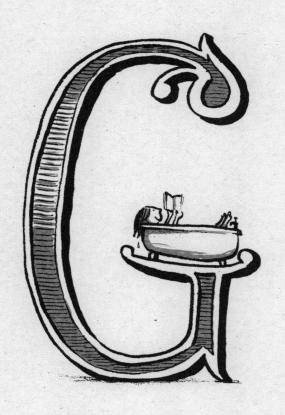

The Powder Monkey

This is the moment I dread,
my eyes sting with smoke,
my ears sing with cannon fire.
I see the terror rise inside me,
coil a rope in my belly to keep it down.
I chant inside my head to freeze my nerve.

Main mast, mizzen mast, foremast,
belfry, capstan, waist.

We must keep the fire coming.
If I dodge the sparks
my cartridge will be safe,
if I learn my lessons
I can be a seaman,
if I close my eyes to eat my biscuit
I will not see the weevils.

Main mast, mizzen mast, foremast,
shot lockers, bowsprit, gripe.

Don't stop to put out that fire,
run to the hold,
we must fire at them
or they will fire at us.

Main mast, mizzen mast, foremast,
belfry, capstan, waist.

My mother never knew me,
but she would want to know this –
I can keep a cannon going,
I do not need her kiss.

CHRISSIE GITTINS

Before 1794 children aged 6 upward went to sea.
After 1794 the minimum age was 13.

Limpet

I am a Cornish limpet,
been here for a hundred years,
sucking and gripping and sticking to this stone
with a hundred thousand fears.

What if I get put in a bucket
and dumped in the boot of a car,
with wellies and jellies and a windbreaker
and a shell in the shape of a star?

I'd miss my chats with the ancient crab,
the swell and wash of the tide,
the soothing stroke of anemones,
the storms when the fish come and hide.

But I hang on tight and hope for the best,
I avoid anyone with a spade,
when the sun beats down in a glisten
on the sea, my fears begin to fade.

CHRISSIE GITTINS

The Living Room

I looked round the room. It was empty.
Hush . . . Nothing. Nobody at home –
    like a wet afternoon
    or a song with no tune,
        like a shrivelled balloon
        or a week on the moon.
And yet . . . no, I wasn't alone.

It may be the way things were standing,
how the floor creaked its one wonky board,
    or the curious feeling
    that up on the ceiling
        I heard a small voice
        from the paint that was peeling
Say *Nothing likes being ignored.*

It said *Everything wants to be something.*
The bracket that once held a shelf –
    just one of it,
    blatantly one of a pair,
        now useless and loose
        but mysteriously *there* –
whispered: *Thanks, I can speak for myself.*

Because nothing is ever quite silent.
You've just never listened before.

The grate of the stool
that you pull up to sit
   says *I'm not a thing.*
   I'm a Me, not an It.
And who ever thinks of the floor?

Everything wants to be something.
Nothing likes being ignored.
   The butter knife
   in the back of the drawer
      that hasn't been used
         since the Second World War
still dreams it's a samurai sword.
And nothing's too dull to be mentioned
And nothing's too worn out to care.
   It may be hard
   and scuffed and scarred
   but the big old baggy-
   robed bum of a bard
once sat in this battered old chair.

And *Scratch me!* whispers the paper.
I've got secrets I don't want to hide.
   Depend on me,
      says the rusty old hook.
         The window says *Look!*
         (and so does the book).
there's a whole wide world outside.

And the put-upon lumpy-stuffed sofa
keeps history deep in its cracks –
     like a crossword, half done,
     and a pink plastic gun
          and a lottery ticket
          that just might have won
              and a raisin or two
              from a ten-year-old bun
and other mouth-watering snacks.

Because everything wants to be something
and everywhere could be explored.
     That small speck of mould
     has a tale to unfold
          about what it's like
          being lonely and old
     and the 100 watt light
     might look happy and bright
          but it may be afraid
          to be switched off at night
     and the phone in the hall
     has a friend it can't call
          but nothing at all,
          be it huge, be it small,
nothing likes being ignored.

PHILIP GROSS

White Ones

with small scritchety claws
and pink
shortsighted blink-
ing–in–the–sunlight
eyes that looked raw
as if they'd cried all night . . .

One morning they were gone.

On holiday,
says Dad. *Gone to stay*
with their friends
in the pet shop. And so I pretend
I don't know about the cage door
he left open. I try to ignore

the look on the face of the cat.

It isn't that
wakes me up in the darkness. No,
it's the scritch and the scratch
at the bars, those pink–eyed
lies. They're only little
white ones, oh

but watch them breed and grow.

PHILIP GROSS

The World is a Box

My heart is a box of affection.
My head is a box of ideas.
My room is a box of protection.
The past is a box full of years.

The future's a box full of after.
An egg is a box full of yolk.
My life is a box full of laughter.
And the world is a box full of folk.

SOPHIE HANNAH

Early Bird Blues

I am the early bird.
I have worn out my shoes
Simply because I heard
First come was first to choose.
One of my talents is avoiding queues.

I never ask how long
I shall be made to wait.
I have done nothing wrong.
I don't exaggerate.
To state the obvious, I'm never late.

Why has the queue not grown?
Nobody hears me speak.
I stand here all alone
Which makes me look unique
But even so, the worm avoids my beak.

What do the others know?
Have I been told a lie?
Why don't I turn and go?
I still know how to fly,
But, damn, I want that worm. I don't know why.

SOPHIE HANNAH

My Dad's Book

Tonight at our house is pirates' night
Not silly costumes with scratchy beards
Rubber swords and a blow-up parrot
No, I mean the real thing.

Dad appears with the ancient book
It's covered in signs and silver stars
Creaking and dusty in battered green leather
He opens it up and it starts to glow.

We sit in the circle and Dad says the words
We shiver and tingle, the air grows warmer
Suddenly thick slices of moonbeams
Stream through the window, solid as stairs.

Up we climb, real pirates
There is our ship anchored in clouds
And away we sail on another adventure
Until the morning flies us home.

Yesterday we cleaned up Dodge City
The day before we flew to Saturn
Last week I scored the cup-final winner
Mum and Dad danced in a famous film.

You can join us, all you need
Is the ancient book with the right words
I'll see you out there, dancing through moonlight
Until the morning flies us home.

DAVID HARMER

South to North; 1965

I was born south of the river
down in the delta, beyond the bayou
lived in the swamps just off the High Street
London alligators snapping my ankles.

It was Bromley, Beckenham, Penge, Crystal Palace
where the kids said *wotcha*, ate bits of *cike*,
the land my father walked as a boy
the land his father walked before him.

I was rooted there, stuck in the clay
until we drove north, moved to Yorkshire
a land of cobbles, coal pits and coke works
forges and steel, fires in the sky.

Where you walked through fields around your village
didn't need three bus-rides to see a farm.

It was Mexbrough, Barnsley, Sprotbrough, Goldthorpe
I was deafened by words, my tongue struck dumb
gobsmacked by a language I couldn't speak in.

Ayop, sithee, it's semmers nowt
What's tha got in thi snap, chaze else paze?
Who does tha support, Owls else Blades?

Dun't thee tha me, thee tha thi sen
Tha's a rate 'un thee, giz a spice?

Cheese and peas, sweets and football
I rolled in a richness of newfound vowels
words that dazed, dazzled and danced
out loud in my head until it all made sense
in this different country, far away
from where I was born, south of the river.

DAVID HARMER

The Painting Lesson

'What's THAT, dear?'
asked the new teacher.

'It's Mummy,' I replied.

'But Mums aren't green and orange!
You really haven't TRIED.
You don't just paint in SPLODGES –
You're old enough to know
You need to THINK before you work . . .
Now – have another go.'

She helped me draw two arms and legs,
A face with sickly smile,
A rounded body, dark brown hair,
A hat – and, in a while,
She stood back (with her face bright pink):
'That's SO much better – don't you think?'

But she turned pale
When, at ten to three,
An orange-green blob
Collected me.

'Hi, Mum!'

TREVOR HARVEY

Favouritism

When we caught measles
It wasn't fair –
My brother collected
Twice his share.

He counted my spots:
'One hundred and twenty!'
Which sounded to me
As if I had plenty.

Then I counted his –
And what do you think?
He'd two hundred and thirty-eight,
Small, round and pink!

I felt I'd been cheated
So 'Count mine again!'
I told him, and scowled
So he dared not complain.

'One hundred and twenty' –
The same as before . . .
In our house, he's YOUNGEST
And he ALWAYS gets *more*!

Trevor Harvey

Did I, Dad?

Dad,
Did I ever say how glad
I am to have you?
What about you, Mum?
No?
How dumb
How mad.

JOHN HEGLEY

Listen

Mum and Dad, I'm feeling sad
let me tell you why,
there's a girl at school
I love up to the sky
but I don't know what she thinks.
I want to say she's elegant
and other words I cannot spell
but I just tell her
she stinks.
I want to be nice to her
but I'm horrible instead,
can I have some advice please,
and another slice of bread.

JOHN HEGLEY

What Is the Pond Doing?
(for Ruairidh, who asked)

Wobbling like a wobbly jelly
Being a bucket for the rain
Sending flash-backs to the sun
Cheeking the sky
Giving the moon a bath
Letting swans, ducks and winter leaves ride on its back
Licking the lollipop reeds
Pretending to be soup for the wind to stir
Growing stinky skunk cabbages
Drawing wheels and circles then rubbing them out
Plopping slopping slurping spinning
Turning the weeping willows happily upside down
Dreaming of running away to sea
Hiding under a starry blanket of dark

What is the pond doing?
Ponding. Responding.

DIANA HENDRY

The Spare Room

It was just the spare room
the nobody there room
the spooks-in-the-air room
the unbearable spare room.

It wasn't the guest room
the four-poster best room,
the designed-to-impress room,
the unuseable guest room.

It wasn't the main room,
the homely and plain room,
the flop-on-the-bed room,
Mum and Dad's own room.

It wasn't the blue room
the sweet lulla-loo room
the creep-on-your-feet room
the baby's asleep room.

It wasn't the bright room
the clothes everywhere room
the music-all-night room
sister's scattered-about room.

It was just the spare room
the nobody there room
the spooks-in-the-air room
the unbearable spare room.

DIANA HENDRY

Rain Falls Down

The clouds begin to rub together
soft as the stroke of a silky feather
then the rain begins to fall

the rain falls down
like tip tip tapping
the rain falls down
like clap clap clapping
and the rain comes falling down

the rain falls down
tumbling under
the rain falls down
like the sound of thunder
and the rain comes falling down

the rain comes down
like the sound of thunder
the rain falls down
tumbling under
and the rain comes falling down

the rain falls down
like the sound of clapping
the rain falls down

like tip tap tapping
and the rain comes falling down

the clouds begin to rub together
soft as the stroke of a silky feather
and the SUN comes out again

MARGOT HENDERSON

Cow in the Cornflakes

Mum, there's a cow in my cornflakes.
Don't be silly, darling, how could a cow fit in?
Mum, there is a cow in my cornflakes.
It's the cow the milk was in.

Mum, there's sea in my fish fingers.
Don't be silly, darling, a sea couldn't possibly fit in.
Mum, there is a sea in my fish fingers.
It's the sea the fish swam in.

Mum, there's a farmer in my egg cup
He fed the hen the grain.
Mum, there's a cloud in your tea cup
It was the cloud that held the rain.

Mum, everything's in everything
It's all joined up together
There's a mountain in my sand pit
And a whole sky in a feather.

MARGOT HENDERSON

Arundel Swimming Pool

is good fun
for everyone –

teetery toddlers
bald dawdlers
and ancient waddlers
keen lean chaps
in goggles and skull-caps
counting the laps –

it's great
for two-yard dashers
unnecessary splashers
crawlers sprawlers
screamers dreamers
bare-back riders
sun-lotioned idlers
backwards-down-the-sliders
drop-outs on loungers
tiny ice-cream scroungers –

it's so smashing for everyone
with all the slosh
and swirl and splash
and shouting friendly din
and the view of the castle

and blue sky now and again
and clouds and swallows and martins
skimming in –

they're going to close it
and turn it into an *Important*
perhaps *Significant*
possibly *Exclusive and Prestigious*
or even *Significantly and Prestigiously Exclusive*

DEVELOPMENT

and instead of an old swimming pool
which is only good fun for everyone
they'll have something to make a lot of money
for someone.

Robert Hull

Sound Count Down

turn of a tap
clicking cap

pulled plug
clinked mug

slowing trickle
final gurgle

squirt of spray
towel put away

cupboard door squeak
basket creak

something picked off the floor
opening door —

can it be
the bathroom's free?

ROBERT HULL

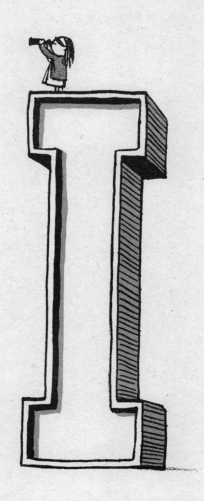

I am a poet
and here's my poem:

'I wrote a poem.
It's by I.
I am a poet
and my name is I.'

by
I

Poem for a Town Child

My dad took me to look in a shop window
Because it was going to be my birthday.
In it there was everything round:
There was a round pot made of a thin stripy snake
Like the ones we did at school, only better.
There was a round mat made of round thin rope
Like the one my sister brought home that I
    thought was good
Only the shop one was not so hairy.
There was a round glass ball on a stand with
    things inside
That seemed to change when you moved your
    head down to look
And I wanted that more than anything
Only my dad said it was very expensive
But the best of all was the roundest thing there
It was a snail and it was round all the way round
And whenever you started to go round it you had
    to go on to the top
And then back round again you couldn't stop
Till your eye reached where you began. It was
    like a puzzle
And much better done than the coily pots and the
    twisty mats though they were good
But my dad said it was part of the decoration, not
    for sale

And anyway he wanted to buy me a present,
    not an old snail
That you could find any time in the yard
But that was the best thing there and that was
    what I wanted
And I thought if we went in and I said that to
    the man
He might give me one
But my dad didn't want to.

JENNY JOSEPH

A Silly Song

Ding-dong   the voices in your head
               the voices in your head
Ding-dong   they fall like gold and lead-
               en voices in your head
Sing-song   the flyers in the sky
               wings cutting through the sky
Sing-song   they lift and then they fly
               the voices in your head
Ping-pong   the balls you puff and pat
               the different games you're good at
Ping-pong   the silly words you say
               to lift the heart. Ping-pong.

The sun shoots up the sky
The bird is on the wing
And high high high
Up and down
Rises, falls
Your happy song.

JENNY JOSEPH

Marbles

The tiny silver one is for my sister.
She's smaller than I am, so it's fair.

The cracked one that looks like a cloudy day
I give to the baby. He's too little to care.

Seven glass shooters full of waves
I'll keep for myself. I found them first.

I hide the ruby one in a secret place.
I love it so much, it burns my face.

MICHAEL KAVANAGH

Potions

For warm summer weather
mix a potion of Dandelion and Heather.

For everlasting sweets
mix a potion of Wisteria and beets.

For exploring a forest path
mix a potion of bark and rotten leaf.

For days off school, and playing in snow
mix a potion of Hawthorn and Sloe.

For winters day to pass
mix a potion of Night Shade and frosted grass.

To disappear without a trace
mix a potion of Old Man's Beard and Mace.

To finally get your own room
mix a potion of Rose and Lemon Balm.

For late nights, TV, and staying up
mix a potion of Daffodil and Buttercup.

If you plan to run away
mix a potion of sedge and hay.

But if you're ready to come back home
mix some Snowdrop and Teasel comb.

MICHAEL KAVANAGH

Valentine

I like your dreamy eyes.
I like your strange stories.
I like your soft shy lips.
I like your daft wee ways.
I like your lovely hands.
I like your snort of a laugh.
I like your witty jokes.
I like your love of gossip.
I like your funny dance.
I like you saying my name.
I like your humble kindness.
I like your lack of shame.
I like you fine. I like you a lot.
Will you be my – you know what?

JACKIE KAY

The Angler's Song

Down where I am, my love, there is no love.
There is no light, no break of day, no rising sun.
Where I am, I call you in; I open my large mouth.
The only light down here comes from my body.

Down where I am is deeper than you imagine.
There is no food, no easy prey, and it is freezing cold.
I sing to make you say my name. My big eyes weep.
This is the world of never-ending darkness, like pain.

Come down. I have been waiting for you a long time.
I wait without appearing to wait.
I see without being seen to see. You know me.
I am big-headed. I am hideous. I am ugly.

Come down. When I find you, I will bite into your belly.
What you see is what you get with me.
There is no other way. I will become you, let us say.
All that will be left of me will be my breathing.

Come down where I am. In and out, out and in.
Down at the very bottom of the deep dark sea.
When I become you, my mouth will stay open.
My open mouth like the river mouth down at the bottom.

Come down where I am. I will flash my lights for you.
My large eyes will take you in, contain you.
I make no promises. I offer nothing. Not even light.
Down, deep down in the dark, at the bottom, is my bed.

My sea bed, love, where there are no promises of love.
Dark – where there are no promises of light.
Where there is little hope of food.
Where day and night are night and day.

My sea bed. I tell no lies so your heart
will not be broken. I offer nothing.
All you will have is my breathing.
But I will give myself up to you.

I will give myself up for you.

JACKIE KAY

First Fire

Until you winked open your eyes, there was only
dark: smooth, featureless, endless.
Until you cried tears so salty, there was no fish-
filled ocean, just a trench of stones and sand.
Until your first breath, there was no perfume, no
flowers or fruit, neither sneezes nor dust.
Until you first got angry, there was no lightning
in the clouds or fear hooked in the heavens.
Until you saw the first fire and it spit sparks,
no stars were in the sky, they had no home to glitter in.
Until your fingers awoke, numbers didn't count,
fists didn't divide and there was no point in adding
    things up.
Until you found ink, all stories, poems and histories
were like water and disappeared so easily.

Until you, was there anything?

JARED LOUCHE

Colour Outside the Lines

I was always told to colour inside the lines,
but sometimes lines just confine your mind.
From somewhere far down in the orange deep
I start to see new colours flowering all around me.
Confusion looks like black static-scrapes
on crinkled, white, burned-edge paper scraps.
Sleep's always coloured deep-ocean green,
rivers of copper tug me through lavender dreams.
Bubblegumblebees swirl from my head
when I'm being silly in bed;
electric red-yellow wasps start to drone
when I'm an angry screaming cyclone.
Thinking hard at doing maths, my head follows
pencil-thin, jagged, rust-red paths.
Shouts are nasty, silver daggers stabbing,
Huge policeman's blue hands grabbing.
Whispers slip out on a crisp, cream strip
with chocolate-brown writing typed across it.
Snores have wide, blazing tiger bands.
Boredom has no colour but fog-grey on wet sand.
Birds chirp chatty, blue paint chips.
Dog barks are cloud-white with dawn-golden sparks.
Trucks rolling by burp grouchy black splashes.

Bicycle bells ring in shaky pink flashes.
Thunder blows a splatter of sickness-green grim,
brushed throughout in a bruised-blue trim.
Boiling kettles make tiny neon-yellow fish that swim.
When I sing a song,
a long string of loud,
rowdy colour explosions
slowly go floating
past my nose and
hilarious horns brightly
pop purple spikes.
Drums' black splashes and
guitars roar orange-red slashes clash,
blue fuzzy bass feathers fly by and
white flecks of dry piano bone-specks
spatter across the mixing mess.
Glorious, glorious, colourful mess,
But music's the colour I love the best.

JARED LOUCHE

My Mate Darren

When I was a kid, my best mate Darren had
a great way of getting his toy soldiers to have a war.
He'd line them up on the kitchen floor,
close the kitchen door, draw the kitchen window blind,
set an alarm clock to ring in one minute's time,
switch off the kitchen light, making the kitchen dark as
    night.
Then he'd take his tennis racquet
and swing it from left to right with all his might
knocking his soldiers everywhere,
sending them flying through the air.
Making them spin – even his dog joined in,
scampering about with a mouthful of toy soldiers
    sticking out.
Then when the alarm clock would ring, whichever side
had the most soldiers still standing would win.
Years later, Darren now a man, strong and big,
was helping his mum bring in a brand new fridge.
When he moved the old one,
he found underneath, in the dirt and the grease
3 toy soldiers who were still fighting the war,
waiting for an enemy that wasn't there anymore.
He dusted them down, stood them gently on the ground
and with as much love as he could,
he told them.
'It's over, you no longer need to be a toy soldier.

You can go back to your wives,
your families and friends you used to know,
lead your former lives. The fighting finished 10 years ago.'
As gently as he could he told them 'there is no more war'.
But no one told his dog,
who ran back in and chewed them up once more.

PAUL LYALLS

Flashback in Winter Light

One Winter just before night,
snow fell so hard it flashed our bit of the world white.
The flakes fell so fast, school sent us home early from class.
As we made our escape from things to be learnt,
we passed the factory gates where they made powdered
   paints.
One of the delivery lorries had crashed, and
the powder paint it was carrying had splashed coloured
   dust
of blue, silver, red and gold, onto the white falling cold.
The powder paint which had made its escape,
embraced the snow crystals to form a new fate.
Water and powder flowed, making rainbow snow.
We made it into walls of blue, silver, red and gold,
until an ice house shimmered in the cold.
We asked our mum if we could sleep in it that night,
and to our delight, she said, 'alright'.
The night was bitter, but inside the rainbow snow house
everything was a glitter.
As we lay down to sleep, out of the dark
came a terrifying noise, rumbling deep.
The sound of the paint factory's machinery creak.
A low growling mix of rattling cries, which brought
   fear to our young eyes.

A grinding noise getting clearer,
angry machinery getting nearer.
We were seized by fear, it was like a dream.
Until I heard my little sister scream,
'It's the paint factory wanting back its dust.'
At that we leapt up and burst through the
    coloured ice,
driven on by a love for life.
Not stopping until we were safe in our beds,
and sleep had melted the vengeful paint
    factory from our heads.
In the morning we went back to see the house
    made of rainbow snow.
Under the sun, its walls still shone, but every
    bit of the colour was gone.
In the distance, the towering paint factory
    blew its whistle and looked on.

PAUL LYALLS

How Was School?

Mum can't see why it's uncool
To ask me cheerfully
'How was school?'
She shakes her head and rolls her eyes
To all of the following replies:

'All right
Not bad
You what?
OK
It went
It was
Couldn't really say
It's dust
It's over
History
Stop nagging will you
What's for tea?
Same stuff
The usual
Can't remember
Ask me again in mid-December
Boring
Pointless
Stupid
Grim

Did some work
Then sang a hymn.'

My mum is such a peculiar creature
She knows how school is
She's the teacher!!

LINDSAY MACRAE

The Wicked Stepmother

I expected her to wear hobnail boots
Beneath a stiff brown skirt.
I expected her to screech
Like a throttled parrot:
'No you can't go to the ball
                              the ball'
Or:
'Scrub that floor again!'

I just knew she would offer me
Shiny, poisoned apples;
Hide all my party invitations;
Spend hours asking the mirror
Leading questions
Then take me into a forest
And leave me there.

I pictured her waiting
For the postman
To deliver a parcel
Containing my torn-out heart.

I thought I would have to
Grow my hair
Until it was long enough
To hang out of high windows

I imagined pinning all my hopes
On a mountaineering prince
Armed with a chainsaw
And a first aid manual.
Or the kindness of seven
Short men.

So imagine my surprise
When an ordinary-looking person arrived
Who likes fairy tales too.

Lindsay MacRae

Me

If I were big
    I'd want to be sky

If I were little
    I'd want to be small elephant

If I were muffin
    I'd want to be chocolate

If I were ice cream
    I'd want to be strawberry (or chocolate)

If I were drink
    I'd want to be fizzy

If I were circus
    I'd want to be clown

If I were summer fair
    I'd want to be bouncy castle

If I were band
    I'd want to be drum

If I were tree
  I'd want to be toffee apple
If I were car
  I'd want to be double-decker bus

If I were water
  I'd want to be sea

If I were someone else
  I'd want to be ME.

ROGER MCGOUGH

The Doll's House

Once upon a not so long ago
a little girl said: 'Build me a doll's house, Daddy.'
'What's the magic word?' said Daddy.
'Please,' said Dorothy.
'That's a good girl,' said Daddy.
And after kissing her goodnight
he turned off the light and went downstairs.

He decided to design and build
the best ever doll's house for his daughter.
It would make her so proud of him.
And so, the very next morning,
he kissed his wife as usual, but instead
of going to work, locked himself in the shed
at the bottom of the garden.

And there he stayed until the days
became weeks and the weeks, months.
At first, he would join the family for meals
but as he explained to his wife
precious time could be saved if she would
be kind enough to leave sandwiches
or a bowl of soup outside his workshop.

After a year, Dorothy's mother begged him,
'If only you would go back to work
we could buy the most expensive doll's house
from the best toy shop in the world.'
'Not good enough for my daughter,' he replied.
'And I'm not coming out until it's finished.'
Then, going back inside, he locked the door.

Years passed.
Sometimes in the middle of the night
Dorothy would creep out of bed,
open the curtains and look out into the garden.
A lamp would be shining in the shed,
and she would see her father silhouetted
against the window like a ghostly shadow puppet.

Years passed.
Dorothy's mother sold the washing machine,
the television, and all the furniture, piece by piece.
She had given up pleading with her husband.
Neither she nor Dorothy saw or spoke to him.
Only heard him hammering and muttering
in his little shed at the bottom of the garden.

Then one morning the door opened
and out stepped an old man, white-haired
and blinking in the sunlight. He called to his wife,
'Tell Dorothy that her doll's house is ready at last.'
But she laughed. 'Oh, you stupid man,

your darling daughter is no longer here.'
The old man trembled, 'What do you mean?'

'I mean that she grew up and left school
and got a good job and met a decent man
and left home to marry and settle down.'
Without a word, the old man turned on his heel,
went back into his workshop and locked the door.
Within days, a For Sale sign was posted outside,
the house was sold and the old lady moved away.

★ ★ ★

A little girl called Anna is playing in the garden
of her new house. She loves the tangled bushes
and the wooden shed, half-hidden by brambles.
There is no key, but one afternoon her father
manages to force the door open with a chisel.
Spiders, beetles, mice scuttle at the intrusion.
And there on a workbench, covered in cobwebs . . .

It has pride of place in her bedroom now,
a magnificent doll's house with plush carpets
on polished floors. Electricity and running water.
In the kitchen, a fridge and a working oven
In the bathroom a jacuzzi. The little girl
knew that no one had played with it before
and considered herself very lucky indeed.

The only thing she didn't like, and which
she quickly threw away, was a doll she found
in the corner of a bedroom with 'Dorothy'
painted on the door. A shrivelled old man,
hands covering his face like a dreadful mask.
Hunched in sorrow. Inconsolable.

ROGER McGOUGH

Cutting My Fingernails

Piles of new moons

In the sink

Fragments of me

Down the plughole

Little smiles

In the tap's waterfall.

Ian McMillan

An Interesting Fact About One of My Relatives

My great great great great great
Great great great great great great
Great great great great great great
Great great great great great
Grandad is very old.

Ian McMillan

The Christmas Shed

It was late afternoon on Christmas Day
with light fading and flakes falling
when the three of us raced through the copse
where rhododendrons and holly bushes
bent low under their burden of fresh snow.
Gasping, we skidded to a stop
at the edge of the estate's allotments.
A bitter, whining wind made us shiver
as it whipped across the frozen earth.
>   *"No one's about.*
>
>   *Come on!"*

Slipping and skating we dashed for Jacko's shed
and at the back crawled through a hole
where the old boards had rotted away.
Inside it was dry. The air was still.
We peered as daylight filtered dimly
through the fly-spattered, cobwebbed window,
and breathed the shed's special smell
of pine, creosote, paraffin, and sawdust.
Fear of discovery made us whisper.
>   *"Let's see if they're*
>
>   *still there."*

Carefully we moved garden implements
that were stacked in a corner.
Dried soil fell and crunched beneath our boots
as we shifted rakes, forks, spades, and hoes,
and *there* was Smoky and her four kittens
warm in a bed of worn gloves and jerseys.
Like the Three Kings we knelt and offered
our Christmas gifts – turkey scraps, ham, a sausage.
Smoky arched and purred and ate hungrily.
        "The kittens
                are still blind."

The food vanished. We watched in silence
as the grey cat lay down and her mewling kittens
guzzled greedily at the milk bar.
                "It's late."
                        We replaced the implements
and crept out of Jacko's old shed.
Like shadows we hared for the cover of the copse.
Chilled to the bone we reached our estate
where Christmas lights were flashing. We split.
        "Same time tomorrow?"
                "Yeah."
                        "See you."

WES MAGEE

The Boneyard Rap

This is the rhythm
of the boneyard rap,
knuckle bones click
and hand bones clap,
finger bones flick
and thigh bones slap,
when you're doing the rhythm
of the boneyard rap.
           Wooooooooo!

It's the boneyard rap
and it's a scare.
Give your bones a shake-up
if you dare.
Rattle your teeth
and waggle your jaw
and let's do the boneyard rap
once more.

This is the rhythm
of the boneyard rap,
elbow bones clink
and backbones snap,
shoulder bones chink
and toe bones tap,

when you're doing the rhythm
of the boneyard rap.
      Wooooooooo!

It's the boneyard rap
and it's a scare.
Give your bones a shake-up
if you dare.
Rattle your teeth
and waggle your jaw
and let's do the boneyard rap
once more.

This is the rhythm
of the boneyard rap,
ankle bones sock
and arm bones flap,
pelvic bones knock
and knee bones zap,
when you're doing the rhythm
of the boneyard rap.
      Wooooooooo!

WES MAGEE

The Woman of Water

There once was a woman of water
Refused a Wizard her hand
So he took the tears of a statue
And the weight from a grain of sand
And he squeezed the sap from a comet
And the height from a cypress tree
And he drained the dark from midnight
And he charmed the brains from a bee
And he soured the mixture with thunder
And he stirred it with ice from hell
And the woman of water drank it down
And she changed into a well

There once was a woman of water
Who was changed into a well
And the well smiled up at the Wizard
And down down down that old Wizard fell

ADRIAN MITCHELL

Yes

A smile says: Yes.
A heart says: Blood.
When the rain says: Drink,
The earth says: Mud.

The kangaroo says: Trampoline.
Giraffes say: Tree.
A bus says: Us,
While a car says: Me.

Lemon trees say: Lemons.
A jug says: Lemonade.
The villain says: You're wonderful.
The hero: I'm afraid.

The forest says: Hide and Seek.
The grass says: Green and Grow.
The railway says: Maybe.
The prison says: No.

The millionaire says: Take.
The beggar says: Give.
The soldier cries: Mother!
The baby sings: Live.

The river says: Come with me.
The moon says: Bless.
The stars say: Enjoy the light.
The sun says: Yes.

ADRIAN MITCHELL

Adrian Mitchell Educational Health Warning!
None of Adrian Mitchell's poems to be used
in connection with any examinations whatsoever!

My Hat!

Here's my hat.
It holds my head,
the thoughts I've had
and the things I've read.

It keeps out the wind.
It keeps off the rain.
It hugs my hair
and warms my brain.

There's me below it,
the sky above it.
It's my lid.
And I love it.

TONY MITTON

I Wanna Be a Star

I wanna be a star.
I wanna go far.
I wanna drive around
in a big red car.
I said yeah yeah yeah
I wanna be a star.

I wanna be a hit.
I wanna be it.
I wanna see my name
all brightly lit.
I said yeah yeah yeah
I wanna be a hit.

I wanna be the scene.
I wanna be on screen.
I wanna make the cover
of a magazine.
I said yeah yeah yeah
I wanna be the scene.

I wanna be a star.
I wanna be a star.
But I've only got a job

in a burger bar —
so far . . .

TONY MITTON

The Shoes

These are the shoes
Dad walked about in
When we did jobs
In the garden,
When his shed
Was full of shavings,
When he tried
To put the fence up,
When my old bike
Needed mending,
When the car
Could not get started,
When he got up late
On Sunday.
These are the shoes
Dad walked about in
And I've kept them
In my room.

These are not the shoes
That Dad walked out in
When we didn't know
Where he was going,
When I tried to lift
His suitcase,
When he said goodbye

And kissed me,
When he left his door-key
On the table,
When he promised Mum
He'd send a postcard,
When I couldn't hear
His special footsteps.
These are not the shoes
That Dad walked out in
But he'll need them
When he comes back home.

JOHN MOLE

The Blackout

I woke to a darkness as absolute
As the end of the world in a Sunday suit.

No luminous ribbon beneath the door,
No pool of moonlight on the floor.

I groped for the lamp beside my bed
But found only empty air instead,

Nothing to tell me where I might be,
Nothing but nothing but nothing to see,

No familiar shape, no shape at all.
I reached up behind me to touch the wall

But just like the lamp it wasn't there,
Only more cavernous empty air.

And then I remembered, not a moment too soon,
That this wasn't home, this wasn't my room

But a hotel bed on the first night away
Of our family seaside holiday

So I waited until the dark stepped back
To put on a lighter shade of black

Then took one huge breath, triumphantly deep,
Plumped up my pillow and went to sleep.

JOHN MOLE

Spider-swallowing

This may be something you do not know,
indeed, it may be something you do not wish
   to know,
but you are, almost certainly,
a spider swallower.

You don't know it's happening,
but be assured, it does.

It's easy to swallow mozzies or midges or flies,
you open your mouth to shout out something
   to your mates
and then before you know it,
something takes a nose dive
down the black hole of your throat.

But spider-swallowing happens at night.

Fast asleep, you're on your back, mouth open,
when a spider that's been happily exploring
   your ceiling
suddenly sees your face from above and lets
   down a line.

Seeing the open trapdoor of your mouth, it thinks,
'I'll just slip inside.'

And at that moment when you feel something
    tickle your teeth,
your mouth snaps shut.

Then there's only one place for the spider to hide
so it carries on down into your insides
never to be seen again.

When you wake next morning you don't
    remember a thing,
but the fact is, **everyone swallows at least eight
    spiders in one lifetime!**

BRIAN MOSES

Shopping Trolley

Scoot down the aisles
in my shopping trolley,
I could go for miles
in my shopping trolley.

Never say excuse me,
never say please,
ram it in the back
of someone's knees.

You really won't
believe your eyes,
my shopping trolley's
been customised.

It's got bull bars,
radio controls,
engine in the back
and it purrs like a Rolls.

It's got a Volvo chassis,
a velvet seat,
and around the store
it can't be beat.

It does somersaults
and big backflips.
roly-polys
and wheely dips.

It does over seventy
miles per hour,
flashing past
in a burst of power.

Scoot down the aisles
in my shopping trolley,
I could go for miles
in my shopping trolley.

Never say excuse me,
never say please,
ram it in the back
of someone's knees.

BRIAN MOSES

Sea-Rock

Sea rock us to love
    rock us to love

Breeze glad us to touch
    glad us to touch

Sun shift us in strides
    shift us in strides

Trees keep the gold and green of memory
    keep the gold and green of memory

But most of all sea
    rock us to love
    rock us to love

GRACE NICHOLS

My Gran Visits England

My gran was a Caribbean lady
As Caribbean as could be
She came across to visit us
In Shoreham by the sea.

She'd hardly put her suitcase down
when she began a digging spree
Out in the back garden
To see what she could see

And she found:
That the ground was as groundy
That the frogs were as froggy
That the earthworms were as worthy

That the weeds were as weedy
That the seeds were as seedy
That the bees were as busy
as those back home

And she paused from her digging
And she wondered
And she looked at her spade
And she pondered

Then she stood by a rose
As a slug passed by her toes
And she called to my dad
as she struck pose after pose,

'Boy, come and take my photo – the place cold,
But wherever there's God's earth, I'm at home.'

GRACE NICHOLS

Goodwin Sands

I have seen the pale gulls circle
against a restless sky;
I have heard the dark winds crying
as dusk-drawn clouds wheel by.

But the waiting waves still whisper
of shadowy ocean lands,
of twisting tides and of secrets
that lie beneath the Sands.

I have seen the wild weed's tangle
and smelt the salted squall;
I have seen the moon rise from the seas,
and felt the long night's fall.

But whose are the voices that echo
from the shifting ocean lands,
that tell of secrets buried
beneath the drifting Sands?

For many sail the Goodwins
and some return to shore;
but others ride in the falling tide
and those are seen no more.

And voices rise from the waters
beneath a restless sky:
in the dying light of coming night
the long-lost sailors sigh;
from the watery lands of Goodwin Sands
I hear the sailors cry.

JUDITH NICHOLLS

Winter

Winter crept
through the whispering wood,
hushing fir and oak;
crushed each leaf and froze each web —
but never a word he spoke.

Winter prowled
by the shivering sea,
lifting sand and stone;
nipped each limpet silently —
and then moved on.

Winter raced
down the frozen stream,
catching at his breath;
on his lips were icicles,
at his back was death.

JUDITH NICHOLLS

Empty House

I hate our house when there's no one in
I miss my family and I miss the din.
The rooms and the hallway seem cold and bare
And the silence hangs like dust in the air.
What's that sound upstairs that makes me start
Driving Fear like an icicle through my heart?
I'm imagining things, there's nobody there –
But I have to make sure so I creep up the stair
I stand holding my breath by the bedroom door
And hear something rustling across the floor.
Then a scratching sound, a tiny cry!
I can't seem to breathe, my throat is dry.
In the silence I hear my own heart beating
And the rumble of water in the central heating.
I should go in but I just don't dare
So I call aloud, 'Is anyone there?'
Nobody answers. I push open the door.
A fluttering shadow crosses the floor.
And now I see him, now understand
And I gather him gently in my hands.
'I won't hurt you, my friend. Don't flutter, don't start.'
But his body beats wild like a feathered heart.
Out through the window, watch him wheel and fly
Carrying my fear across the sky.

GARETH OWEN

Bedmobile

I hear my grandad on the stair
He's counting, One Two Three
Bringing a rosy apple plucked
From my special climbing tree.
He brings the garden in with him
The flowers and the air
And there are twigs and petals
Tangled in his hair.
And as I eat my apple
He sits down next to me
Turning an imaginary wheel.
'Where to today?' says he.
And we drive our deluxe Bedmobile
To school along the heath
With the apple dribbling sweetness
Clenched between my teeth.

GARETH OWEN

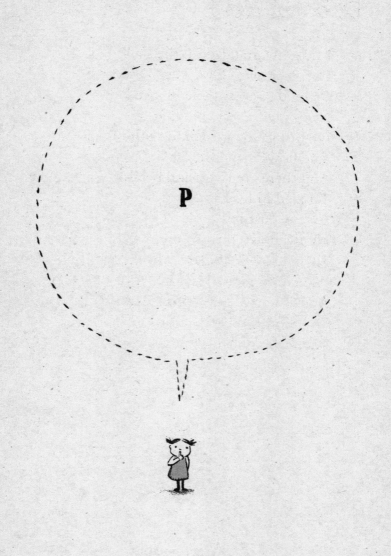

Geography Lesson

Our teacher told us one day he would leave
And sail across a warm blue sea
To places he had only known from maps,
And all his life had longed to be.

The house he lived in was narrow and grey
But in his mind's eye he could see
Sweet-scented jasmine clinging to the walls,
And green leaves burning on an orange tree.

He spoke of the lands he longed to visit,
Where it was never drab or cold.
I couldn't understand why he never left,
And shook off the school's stranglehold.

Then halfway through his final term
He took ill and never returned.
He never got to that place on the map
Where the green leaves of the orange trees burned.

The maps were pulled down from the classroom wall,
His name was forgotten, it faded away.
But a lesson he never knew he taught
Is with me to this day.

I travel to where the green leaves burn,
To where the ocean's glass-clear and blue,
To all the places my teacher taught me to love
But which he never knew.

Brian Patten

The Boy Who Broke Things

The boy kept breaking things.
He broke the one window through which the world
　　looked bright.
He broke bottles.
He broke promises.
He broke his mother's heart.
He broke the lock on the cupboard in which she kept
　　the sky,
And so she floated off,
And was lost amongst clouds forever.
He broke the lock on the box in which his father kept
　　the ocean.
His father was swept away and drowned,
And the boy never saw him again.
Angry, he stomped on the earth and tried to break it,
But it was a tough nut, the earth –
Far tougher than him.
And his anger grew,
Until it became a tree inside him,
And all its leaves were poisonous, and nothing sang,
And all its branches were empty.
The boy was angry.
He tore the curtain that separated life from death,

And so he could no longer tell
What was living and what was dead inside him.
He smashed the clues we use to separate fact
    from fiction,
They became one thing to him.
His anger was like a nasty giant.
He was angry, but he could not say why.
The answer to his anger stuck in his throat
It was a secret he did not want to keep, but could
    not get rid of,
And the bottled up pain inside him was like a
    mad genie.
And he wept, and he wept and he wept.

BRIAN PATTEN

School Trip

On our school trip to Scarborough
We got to school on time,
But the coach was caught in traffic
And arrived at half past nine.
Miss Phipps, our teacher, was so cross,
Left standing in the rain
And when the coach pulled up at last
She didn't half complain.
The driver started shouting,
He said there'd been a queue,
But Miss Phipps she said, 'That's no excuse!'
And started shouting too.

On our school trip to Scarborough
The sky turned cold and grey,
Freezing winds blew down the beach
And it rained and rained all day.
Then Sharon slipped on a slimy rock,
And Gordon grazed his knee,
And Colin fell off the castle wall,
And John jumped in the sea.
Then our teacher started shouting
And her voice was loud and high,
And soon we were surrounded
By a crowd of passers-by.

On our school trip to Scarborough
There was really quite a do
When Hazel's hat blew out to sea
And Simon lost a shoe,
And David dropped his flask of soup
Which rolled right off the pier
And landed on the coastguard
Who happened to be near.
Then the coastguard started shouting
When it hit him with a **thwack**
And when David said, 'I'm sorry, mate,
Could you pass my thermos back?'

On our school trip to Scarborough
We all ate tons and tons
Of sticky rock and sandwiches
And jellied eels and buns.
And when the coach left Scarborough
Sam was sick on Chris
And Chris was sick on Wayne and Paul
And they were sick on Miss.
Then everyone was shouting
All the children and Miss Phipps
Until Jason asked the driver,
'Can we stop for fish and chips?'

On our school trip to Scarborough
It wasn't that much fun,
Nothing really happened

And we never saw the sun.
We couldn't do a lot of things
Because of all the rain,
But if I have the chance next year
I'd love to go again!

GERVASE PHINN

Late Home

Mum: And where have you been until this time?

Boy: I was . . .

Mum: Playing football, I bet.

Boy: No, I was . . .

Mum: When you should have come straight home.

Boy: If I could explain . . .

Mum: The times I tell you . . .

Boy: You see, I was . . .

Mum: To come straight home.

Boy: But . . .

Mum: You just don't listen, do you?

Boy: I do, but . . .

Mum: In one ear and out the other.

Boy: But . . .

Mum: No more buts, young man.

Boy: You see . . .

Mum: Now, go and wash your hands.

Boy: I'm trying to tell you . . .

Mum: Tea will be on the table in five minutes.

Boy: The thing is . . .

Mum: Have you any homework?

Boy: Yes, I have, but . . .

Mum: Well, after tea it's up to your room.

Boy:	Could I explain . . .
Mum:	And no television tonight.
Boy:	I'm trying to tell you . . .
Mum:	Don't just stand there.
Boy:	Will you listen, please?
Mum:	Do as you're told!
Boy:	Mrs Wilson!!!!!
Mum:	Pardon?
Boy:	I've been trying to tell you!
Mum:	What?
Boy:	That I am not your son and you're not my mum.
Mum:	Oh!
Boy:	I live next door.

GERVASE PHINN

Magpie

The magpie weaves into its nest
what the magpie likes the best.

Two rusty pieces of barbed wire;
three dusty coals from an old gas fire.
The charred stump of a table leg;
the bejewelled dagger of a Tuareg.

The magpie weaves into its nest
what the magpie likes the best.

The warm slant of a summer sun;
the worn stock of a broken gun.
One liquorice-y Wellington boot;
one playground bin of drained Fruit Shoots.

The magpie weaves into its nest
what the magpie likes the best.

The scree that falls from a castle rock;
the tail-feathers of a turkey-cock.
The loose change from a taxi driver;
the bubbles from a Dead Sea diver.

The magpie weaves into its nest
what the magpie likes the best.

A flame from the fire-eater's fire;
the brazenness of an out and out liar.
An earring filched from a craft stall;
The pinkish eye of a plastic doll.

The shining skin of a Brussels Sprout;
the laughter of queues going in and out.
A lock of hair from Rapunzel's tower;
Princes Street in an August shower.

The magpie weaves into its nest
what the magpie likes the best.

A tent of children, stair on stair;
poetry's rythems, layer on layer.

The magpie weaves into its nest
what the magpie likes the best.

And what the magpie likes the best
is to welcome us all into its nest.

TOM POW

Where's Nellie?

Gary, Sally, Nick and Nellie
went down to the beach one day;
said Gary to Sally and Nick,
'Come on, let's start to play!'

Gary and Sally ran like horses,
kicking at the white, white foam;
Nick held to their waist bands
and guided them both back home

to a sand castle that stood
with turrets topped by shells.
Building those walls was not such fun
as watching while they fell!

But where was Nellie?

Nellie was crouched in a rock pool,
turning a shell between her hands.
When the sunlight caught it,
it reflected pearly bands.

But even more marvellous,
apart from a trace of sand,
a tiny creature lived there –
pink, with claws and feathery hands.

Oh but come on Nellie!

Gary, Sally, Nick and Nellie
went down to the woods one day;
said Gary to Sally and Nick,
'Well, what shall we play?'

They hid behind tall fir trees,
they sailed on a branch of oak.
Gary and Sally were pirates now,
Nick was for the long deep soak.

But Nick – he had other ideas!
King of the deep green seas,
his very own sea monster brought
Gary and Sally to their knees.

But where was Nellie?

Nellie was squatting in a clearing,
catching sunlight in her hands;
and as it trickled on her skin
it looked like golden sand.

Then she bent over a toadstool
and poked a spider with a stick;
and every time she used it,
the spider ran all over it.

Oh but come on Nellie!

Gary, Sally, Nick and Nellie
went down to the park one day;
said Gary to Sally and Nick,
'Well, what shall we play?'

They started on the roundabout
till Gary felt quite sick.
Round and round and round they went –
Sally couldn't get enough of it!

Then they went down the slide,
polishing it again and again;
Gary, then Sally, then Nick,
together hooting like a train.

But where was Nellie?

Nellie was covered with pigeons
that would not go away;
she held handfuls of crumbs
                    and stood very still
like St Francis of Assisi:

the one who talked to birds
like Nellie liked to do. *Croo-croo*
went an armful of pigeons,
to which Nellie replied, *Croo-croo.*

Oh but come on Nellie!

Gary, Sally, Nick and Nellie
went to a party one day;
said Gary to Sally and Nick,
'Well what shall we play?'

'Hang on there,' said Sally,
'*Where's Nellie?*'

Gary, Sally and Nick
turned themselves about,
but before they could open their mouths,
they heard the loudest shout —

**'Right behind you.
I'm not STUPID!'**

TOM POW

Q here for the poet.

Get in line.
No pushing.

Invaders

Celts wore kilts,
Romans had omens,
The Viking had a liking for hiking.

Goths wore cloths,
Moguls were scared of bogles,
Vandals strolled in sandals.

Anglo-Saxons put their Ankle-Soxon

JOHN RICE

Dazzledance

I have an eye of silver,
I have an eye of gold,
I have a tongue of reed-grass
and a story to be told.

I have a hand of metal,
I have a hand of clay,
I have two arms of granite
and a song for every day.

I have a foot of damson,
I have a foot of corn,
I have two legs of leaf-stalk
and a dance for every morn.

I have a dream of water,
I have a dream of snow,
I have a thought of wildfire
and a harp-string long and low.

I have an eye of silver,
I have an eye of gold,
I have a tongue of reed-grass
and a story to be told.

JOHN RICE

Noises in the Night

Who's that running down the tenement stair?
Only Murdo's mammy with the ginger hair.

Who's that clumping up above my head?
Only Bobby Boddle, who should be in his bed.

What's that scratching on the window-pane?
Only Mr Teagle's cat, trying to get in.

What's that gushing like very heavy rain?
Only Jessie's bathwater rushing down the drain.

What's that buzzing, will it ever stop?
Only Jock the watchman's old alarm clock.

What's that click and snuffle and bleep?
Only your imagination. Go to sleep!

DILYS ROSE

Day-old Stubble

Hubble, bubble,
froth and scrubble,
I watch Dad soap
his day-old stubble.

He sloshes on foam
then scrapes it clean
and rinses his cheeks
of shaving cream.
He splashes his face
with ice-cold water,
pats it dry
with a towel blotter.
Then – he says it's not scent
but he can't fool me –
he scooshes his chin
with a perfumed spray.
Now Dad's ready
to face the day.

Hubble, bubble,
froth and scrubble,
I'm glad Dad's got rid
of his scratchy old stubble.

DILYS ROSE

The Difference

In Glasgow
the hotel gave us something called
'Soap'.
In Edinburgh
the hotel gave us the same stuff
and it was called:
'Skincare Bar'.

MICHAEL ROSEN

The Noise

If my father wanted you to be quiet
he didn't say, shhh,
he didn't say, be quiet
he didn't say, shuttup

All he did was put his hand up
to the side of his face
and say in a quiet voice
that sounded as if
there was some kind of terrible pain
in the middle of his brain
'The noi–i–i–se!'
It was as if the palm of his hand
was trying to reach inside
his head to get at some awful thing in there.

So, we would be going on a car trip.
Dad driving, Mum next to him.
Me and my brother in the back.
My brother says
'There's an imaginary line
down the middle of the back seat.
I'm this side.
You're that side.
You can't cross the line.
I'm this side of the line.

You're that side of the line.
So –'
'Yeah I get the point,' I say,
'there's a line.'
'. . . and you can't cross the line,' he says.
So I say,
'Yeah yeah, I get the point
I won't cross the line.'
And I stick my hand over the line.
'Hey,' he says, 'you crossed the line.'
'I didn't,' I say, and I stick my hand
across the line again.
'YOU CROSSED THE LINE!' he says.
'I DIDN'T,' I say, and I stick my hand
across the line again.
'MUM! HE CROSSED THE LINE!'
'I DIDN'T,' I say.

And my dad's hand goes up
To the side of his face and:
'The noi–i–i–i–se!'

My brother used to imitate it.

If I was making a racket
my brother would walk round the house
saying
'The NOISE! The NOISE!'

So it's breakfast.
My dad couldn't stand any noise
at breakfast.
One sniff
and it was the GLARE.

He comes downstairs
sits down in the chair
and opens up the newspaper.
You can't see him.
He's disappeared.
One moment you've got a dad
and the next you've got a newspaper.

All you see is his hand.
It comes out from behind the newspaper
moves across the table all on its own
finds the cup of coffee
and disappears behind the newspaper.
He didn't even drop the newspaper
to see where the cup was.
He just knew where it was.
We used to stare at the hand
coming out, grabbing the cup
disappearing behind the paper.

Once, my brother
moved the coffee cup.
The hand came out,

couldn't find the cup.
The newspaper came down,
'What's going on?' says my dad.
He grabs the cup
and disappears again behind the paper.

Once, I sat there and a little voice inside me said,
'Hey, why don't you practise playing drums
on the side of the table?'
And I said, 'No, that would be crazy.
Dad can't stand any noise at breakfast.'
And the voice said,
'Yeah, but you know you want to.
Go on. Pick up the knife and fork
and blam blam blam, away you go.'
'No, no, no, I couldn't.'

But I did.
Knife, fork, side of table and
blam blam blam!

The newspaper came down
and my dad's hand went up to the side of his face,
he started to say, 'The no-i–'
But my brother was in there quick
with
'THE NOISE!!!'
And my dad was left there with his

hand in mid-air still trying to say
'The no-i-i-i-i-ise!'

MICHAEL ROSEN

Jellyfish Fuss

When I was a child I stood on a rock
For fear of stepping on jellyfish.

The beach was littered with them
And I feared the sting of the tentacles,
The jelly of the saucers.

The rock was warm and firm;
Like a castle it lifted me above danger.

I closed my eyes, curled up and listened
To distant waves raking the shingle,
And seagulls chuckling, 'Auk-auk-auk.'

The tide was coming in, it was time to move,
But how, when jellyfish waited and wobbled?

Two large hands clasped my waist,
I flew up into the salty air,
Saved by Dad, who picked his way through
    the jellyfish
Like a carnival stilt-walker.

CORAL RUMBLE

Detention Tension (a rap)

I'm looking at the ceiling,
I'm looking at the wall,
I'm looking at the floor
And I'm feeling very small;
I'm in detention,
Just feel the tension,
Teacher's attention
Is all on me.

I'm sitting at a desk,
I'm sitting very still,
I'm sitting up straight
And I'm feeling sort of ill;
I'm in detention,
Just feel the tension,
Teacher's attention
Is all on me.

I'm writing out lines,
I'm writing very fast,
I'm trying to write neatly,
I don't think it will last;
I'm in detention,
Just feel the tension,
Teacher's attention
Is all on me.

I'm trying to look sorry,
I'm trying to look good,
I'm trying to behave
The way I know I should;
I'm in detention,
Just feel the tension,
Teacher's attention
Is all on me.

Now . . .
Teacher's looking at the ceiling,
He's looking at the wall,
He's looking at the floor
And I think he's going to call,
'End of detention,
Can't stand the tension,
'Cause your attention
Is all on me!'

CORAL RUMBLE

The Jealous Ones

Don't look over your shoulder. We're coming soon,
with hungry hands that reach and snap like jaws,
fingers like sharp teeth. We want what's yours

and will not stop until we've pulled it down,
until it's stung by sticks or stones, until it's useless
as a juicy toffee apple stamped into the dirt.

And all because we can. Because your happiness itches
under our skins. And when we have it, tethered, leashed,
we'll roll over ourselves, each of us wanting to be the one

to burst your bright red bubble. But for now, we'll wait
in shadows, watching. You'll feel our eyes on your back.
And when we come for you, you'll hear us,

baying at your pride and joy – the way it floats
beyond us – we'll howl across the distance
as if it were a fat, red, candied moon.

JACOB SAM-LA ROSE

How a Poem Arrives

Sometimes, it's just a beginning,
nothing more, no directions
for where to go next. Sometimes
it arrives like furniture, no instructions
for assembly, no step-by-step.
Sometimes, it's like a dinosaur's bone,
like a key that would open a door
to something bigger, if you knew
where to look for the lock. Sometimes
it calls you, long distance, on a bad line,
and you have to guess every other word.
Sometimes it whispers through your dreams,
then fades in the morning's light.
And sometimes it arrives on your doorstep
like a well-known friend, lets itself in,
sits down at your desk
and writes itself.

JACOB SAM-LA ROSE

There'll Be a Jazz Band

There'll be a jazz band
                    a jazz band swinging
in the big tent we'll hire
                    for their golden wedding

There'll be a jazz band
                    a jazz band swinging
in the big tent we'll hire
                    for their golden wedding

                    & Grandad and Granny
will be scatting & singing
                    she like some old jazzer
he like some old jazzer

                    They'll swing   sing   & scat
to the jazz band swinging

to

                    the

                              jazz band swinging

in the big tent we'll hire
                    for their golden wedding

There'll be a jazz band

          a jazz band swinging

in the big tent we'll hire

          for their golden wedding

FRED SEDGWICK

The Girls in my Class

I love Hannah's hairstyle
And Danuella's dress.
I love Chloe's class – she is
A clear catwalk success –

But Gertie gets me giggling
And I love Gertie best.

I love Rita's writing,
I love Zara's art.
The music plays with Pol
Hammers in my heart –
I hear it from the north, the south,
The east and from the west –

But Gertie gets me giggling
And I love Gertie best.

I love Maggie's movement
When she's jiving in the gym.
I love Sabrina's soft good night
When disco lights are dim.
I love the way that Pippa passes
Every little test –

<u>But Gertie gets me giggling</u>
<u>And I love Gertie best.</u>

I love Eram's glossy hair,
I love Nasima's nose.
I love Farida's fingers
And her brightly painted toes.
I love Niamh and Norma
When I'm feeling sad and stressed –

<u>But Gertie gets me giggling</u>
<u>And I love Gertie best.</u>

FRED SEDGWICK

Reincarnation

I'm
putting my name down
to come back
as a cat
like our Cleo,

I will
snooze
the whole of my next life away,
letting my pride and joy,
my tail,
find the warmest places,

that corner of the garden
the sun lingers in
round the roots of the laburnum,

that spot on the landing
where hot water pipes run
under the carpet;

whenever I want to
I'll stretch myself,
arching my back ecstatically,

dig my fine claws into
the bedside rug,
a plump cushion, someone's lap;

I'll go mooching and mousing
by the light of the moon

and come in any old time I like!

You can guarantee
someone will always
be there

to feed me, stroke me,
make me purr.

MATT SIMPSON

Fifteen Ways of Looking at a Ladybird

a tiny bustling crimson bun
topped with raisins

***

a gaily-coloured brooch
walking on six legs

***

a titchy tinplate clockwork toy,
glossy fire-engine-red

***

or a little old lady
pottering about
tending the garden

***

here's one marching
up the rose stems
to the underside of leaves
tacky with succulent aphids

***

another playing upside-down dead
so's not to get guzzled
by impertinent birds

***

and another squeezing out
a gruesome-tasting liquid
that screams to predators 'Get off!'

***

the bird of Our Lady
in Russia God's cow
in Ireland God's little cow
in Denmark Mary's hen

***

(why aren't there
any lordbirds?)

***

grant us good luck
ask God, on our behalf, to give us
good weather, bring us bread

MATT SIMPSON

Don't You Like Me?

What did I say?

What did I do?

Whatever you heard

it isn't true . . .

PAULINE STEWART

Sometimish Sea

Sometimes the sea is
calm as can be
waves rippling, glittering, peacefully,
sometimes though too
sea seems three shades of blue . . .
pick it up, hold it near
now sea falls free glistening clear
free
as sand
liquid salt between
the hands
Sometimish, stunning, sparkling sea
to and fro quite gracefully –
but if a hurricane should blow
sometimes sea gets cross you know . . .
no more blue slipping quietly by
but heavy leaden,
sea green/grey broody, electric
like stormy sky
sometimish mountainous sea
crashing down scarily,
raging, wrecking and drowning
hurling, whirling, smashing, scowling,
the sea batters and whips along
whistling winds
no singing songs

in its wake
then calm
changes back into a friend
Sometimish sea
Sometimish sea
pure inconsistentsea . . .

PAULINE STEWART

Sea Monsters

Up from the pitsaw they are bringing fresh green boards.
At the window, hand over knotty hand, men pass them in;
each will season for a year. Rain scours the courtyard
as women hurry back and forth in heavy oilskin

capes and hoods. An apprentice shivers by the stable.
The stink of tanning hides wafts down the passageway
from the upholsterer's shop. I will make a table
next. A table so finely jointed, polished and inlaid

it will be a masterpiece. Out on the causeway,
sea serpents attack a cart. Men beat them off with staves.
A comet showed its lustrous tail last night. Some prayed.
Down the coast, another town is ravaged by the plague.

TIM TURNBULL

Yorkshire Day

I'm going to be dour on Yorkshire Day –
I'm going to be extra dour –
and put on me special Yorkshire face;
the one that makes the milk turn sour.

And I'm going to be mardy on Yorkshire Day;
mardy and contrary
and I won't crack a smile all Yorkshire Day.
Laughter is for fairies.

I'm going to be tight on Yorkshire Day;
no brass will leave my clutch
and I'm going to be tacit on Yorkshire Day.
Oh heck. I've said too much.

TIM TURNBULL

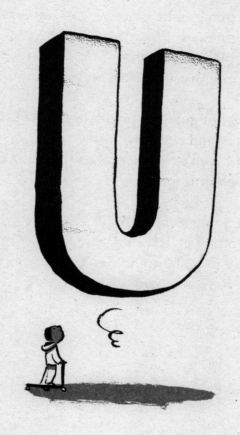

U are a poet
and here is your poem:

V is the Ventriloquist poet.
This page is the Ventriloquist poet's dummy.
I'm sorry but the Ventriloquist poet has left the room.
But the Ventriloquist poet has left behind the dummy.
As the Ventriloquist poet isn't here
U can make the Ventriloquist poet's dummy speak.

I don't think the Ventriloquist will mind.
Not much.
Go on.
I know U want to.

One Boy Stood in the Field

One boy stood in the field alone
The wind blows over
The wind blows back
Nothing grows where the white wind blows
One boy stood in the field

Two boys side by side in the field
The wind blows over
The wind blows back
Nothing grows where the white wind blows
Two boys stood in the field

Three boys planted the field with corn
The wind blows over
The wind blows back
Green shoots grew where the white wind blew
Three boys stood in the field

Four boys pulled the weeds and thorns
The wind blows over
The wind blows back
Tall corn grew where the white wind blew
Four boys stood in the field
A score of boys reaped the golden corn

The wind blows over
The wind blows back
Stacked it up in long straight rows
A score of boys in the field

A hundred millers milled the grain
The wind blows over
The wind blows back
Stored in barns from the cold and rain
A hundred milled the grain

DAVE WARD

Bobby's Bubble Gum

Bobby blew his bubble gum
Big and fat and wide.
Bobby blew his bubble gum
Then swallowed it inside.
The bubble gum swelled up and grew
Inside Bobby's belly
Till Bobby wobbled round the room
Like a bowl of jelly.

Bobby clutched his aching guts,
His Mum began to cry;
Then Bobby sat down on a pin
And POP!
          He hit the sky.

So when you blow your bubble gum
Big and fat and wide:
Let it cover up your grin,
Let it dribble down your chin,
Let it cling on to your skin –
But don't swallow it inside.

DAVE WARD

The Death of a Bully

<u>I'm glad he's gone!</u>

For once I can walk to school feeling free – no eyes on
me

<u>I sigh in relief</u>

The things that I feel I can easily achieve are beyond
belief

<u>I laugh with my friends</u>

When we're out at break time there's no pressure on us
and the fun never ends

CURTIS WATT

My Cat Just Saw a Ghost

My cat just saw a ghost, but I didn't see a thing.
He was sitting on the mat, licking his paws just like a king.
He looked up very sharply with a ghostly gaze and gawk.
It's as though he heard a whisper, but there's no one here
to talk.

I heard a creak behind me, but there's no one here to walk
In this room, on these old flaky floors and creaky,
crooked boards.
So I looked for reassurance in my cat's green, gaping eyes,
But he seemed confused, when usually he was brave and
wise.

His tongue was hung and frozen in a pause from licking
fur.
His ears and whiskers peaked on end, as though stung by
the air.
His tail twitched – flinching rapidly – and razor claws
were clasped.
If he could speak of what he saw, I'd be too scared to ask.

He looked more scared than that small bird he stalked
and killed one day.
I'd throw my cat a ball of wool, but I'm too scared to
play.

He winced at me as though he needed lap time and a
    stroke –
And this was very rare because he's quite a macho bloke.

Did he see a form materialize then vaporize to smoke?
If he could understand, I'd lighten him up with a joke.
I just sat and gripped my chair with a silent, stony stare,
Thinking, *I'm more scared than him so I can't speak or move
    with fear.*

CURTIS WATT

Dave Dirt Was on the 259

Dave Dirt was on the 259
(Down Seven Sisters Road it goes),
And since he'd nothing else to do
He stuck his ticket up his nose,

He shoved his pen-top in his ear,
He pulled three hairs out of his head,
He ate a page out of his book,
He held his breath till he went red,

He stuck his tongue out at the queue,
He found a nasty scab to pick,
He burped and blew a raspberry,
He imitated being sick,

He stuck a piece of bubblegum
Inside a dear old lady's bonnet.
If you should catch the 259,
Make sure that Dave Dirt isn't on it!

KIT WRIGHT

The Magic Box

I will put in the box

the swish of a silk sari on a summer night,
fire from the nostrils of a Chinese dragon,
the tip of a tongue touching a tooth.

I will put in the box

a snowman with a rumbling belly,
a sip of the bluest water from Lake Lucerne,
a leaping spark from an electric fish.

I will put in the box

three violet wishes spoken in Gujarati,
the last joke of an ancient uncle
and the first smile of a baby.

I will put in the box

a fifth season and a black sun,
a cowboy on a broomstick
and a witch on a white horse.

My box is fashioned from ice and gold and steel,
with stars on the lid and secrets in the corners.
Its hinges are the toe joints
of dinosaurs.

I shall surf in my box
on the great high-rolling breakers of the wild Atlantic,
then wash ashore on a yellow beach
the colour of the sun.

KIT WRIGHT

X marks the spot
Where there could be a poet.
Is the poet U?

Y is a poet.

Y is a poet?
I don't know
Y a poet is.
Do U?

People Need People

To walk to
To talk to
To cry and rely on,
People will always need people.
To love and to miss
To hug and to kiss,
It's useful to have other people.
To whom will you moan
If you're all alone,
It's so hard to share
When no one is there,
There's not much to do
When there's no one but you,
People will always need people.

To please
To tease
To put you at ease,
People will always need people.
To make life appealing
And give life some meaning,
It's useful to have other people.
If you need a change
To whom will you turn,
If you need a lesson
From whom will you learn,

If you need to play
You'll know why I say
People will always need people.

As girlfriends
As boyfriends,
From Bombay
To Ostend,
People will always need people.
To have friendly fights with
And share tasty bites with,
It's useful to have other people.
People live in families
Gangs, posses and packs,
It seems we need company
Before we relax,
So stop making enemies
And let's face the facts,
People will always need people,
          Yes
People will always need people.

BENJAMIN ZEPHANIAH

I De Rap Guy

I am de rapping rasta
I rap de lyrics fasta
Dan a Ford Cortina
Or a double ghetto blasta,
When royals are listening
They proclaim me as a king
I am way out an travelling
Not a puppet on a string.

I am de rapping rasta
De lyrical masta
Dey say I am good to go
So I go wid de flow,
If yu really want to know
Yu should book me for a show
I will tek yu high an low
Like an eagle or a roe.

What I spread is unity
Or to put it simply
I want racial harmony
In de world community,
I am big an I am bad
So bad I will mek yu glad
An you'll hav to tell ya Dad
Bout de rapper yu just had.

I rap on de move
Wid a little tongue an groove
Wid ability to soothe
Warmongers may not approve,
I can put yu in your place
Wid a little drum an bass
I am proud of every race
I out ran de steeplechase.

I am de rapping rasta
Flesh an bone not plaster
My ideas are very green
And I keep me rapping clean,
Let me take yu on a tour
I know what I'm rapping for,
I can rap from coast to coast
And I don't like to brag or boast.

Benjamin Zephaniah

Acknowledgements

The editor and publishers gratefully acknowledge permission to reproduce copyright material in this book. Every effort has been made to trace and contact copyright holders, but in a few cases this has proved impossible. The editor and publishers apologize for these unwilling cases of copyright transgression and would like to hear from any copyright holders not acknowledged.

'Chick Pea Pie' and 'Spellbound' by Adisa, copyright © Adisa, 2009, reprinted by permission of the author; 'Laughter Rap in Plastic Town' and 'The Soldiers Came' by John Agard, copyright © John Agard, 1990, reproduced by kind permission of John Agard c/o Caroline Sheldon Agency Ltd; 'The Mighty Slide' by Allan Ahlberg from *The Mighty Slide*, published by Puffin Books 1989, copyright © Allan Ahlberg, 1988, reprinted by permission of Penguin Books Ltd; 'Grrrr' by Francesca Beard from *The Poetry Store*, published by Hodder Children's Books 2005, copyright © Francesca Beard, 2005, reprinted by permission of the author; 'I Speak the Language' by Francesca Beard, copyright © Francesca Beard, 2008, reprinted by permission of the author; 'Air Raids 1942' by Gerard Benson from *To Catch an Elephant*, published by Smith/Doorstop 2002,

278

Index of First Lines